EVERY WOMAN'S Privilege

JOY P. GAGE

MULTNOMAH · PRESS
Portland, Oregon 97266

Other books in this series:

Becoming Complete: Embracing Your Biblical Image
Marion Duckworth
Empty Arms: Emotional Support for Those Who Have Suffered Miscarriage and Stillbirth
Pam Vredevelt
In the Name of Submission: A Painful Look at Wife Battering
Kay Marshall Strom
Walking a Thin Line: Anorexia and Bulimia
Pam Vredevelt and Joyce Whitman
Women Under Stress: Preserving Your Sanity
Randy and Nanci Alcorn

Edited by Liz Heaney

EVERY WOMAN'S PRIVILEGE

Published by Multnomah Press
Portland, Oregon 97266

Multnomah Press is a ministry of Multnomah School of the Bible, 8435 NE Glisan Street, Portland, OR 97220.

Printed in the United States of America

Library of Congress Cataloging-in-Publication Data

Gage, Joy P.
Every woman's privilege.

Includes bibliographical references.
1. Women—Religious life. I. Title.
BV4527.G343 1986 248.8'43 86-23587
ISBN 0-88070-177-3 (pbk.)

86 87 88 89 90 91 92 93 – 8 7 6 5 4 3 2 1

For two special women:
Jurine Cressey Pennock
who gave me life and believed in me
until the day she died
and
Hazel Wigger Pennock
who came afterward,
friend, confidante, encourager,
and loving grandmother to my children

CONTENTS

ACKNOWLEDGMENTS

Special thanks to Liz Heaney who has given new meaning to the word *editor.* Acting as both a sounding board and an adviser, she guided the manuscript from conception to birth.

In addition, I would like to thank Dr. LeRoy Thomas, my first minister, because he had the foresight to encourage spiritual responsibility in young girls who would one day grow up to be women.

INTRODUCTION

Where will today's Christian woman turn for answers while the church makes up its mind about issues that confront her where she lives?

As a speaker who travels frequently, I sometimes find it difficult to put into perspective the problems related to me by Christian women. Even after hearing a version of the same problem in three different states, I still have to ask myself, "Are these isolated incidents or is this a trend? Is this representative of the Christian community or is it a sensational exception?"

I know there are hurting women in our churches . . .

> Women who want to serve the Lord more actively with their spiritual gifts.
>
> Women left out of the decision-making process.
>
> Women whose intelligence and abilities intimidate husbands, co-workers, and friends.
>
> Women living with guilt over a second marriage following a divorce they did not perpetrate.
>
> Women advised by pastors to "endure your husband's adultery as your reasonable sacrifice to save the marriage."

I have talked to counselors who work with abused wives and sexually abused children from Christian homes.

I have concluded that for every major problem confronting women today, there is an unresolved theological debate that affects the solution.

The Christian community is vociferous about the sanctity of marriage, but it is too often silent about the sanctity of a woman's life and the evils of wife abuse. A woman's place of submission in the home is argued frequently, but the problems that arise when a man does not love his wife are seldom acknowledged. A local body of believers may be adamant about what a woman should not do in the church, but few churches are creative or consistent about what she should do.

We can no longer regard these issues as subjects to be debated in the seminary classroom or on the convention floor. We of the Christian community must realize that our inability to understand the correct teaching on these issues is contributing greatly to the pain of women in our churches.

Numerous books have been written to correct error in theology and church practice. Without such books addressed to theologians and church leaders there can be little hope to bring about change. Unfortunately, the printed page does not easily translate into action. The reader will not find consensus among the authors. A woman may be delighted by the position of one writer only to discover conflicting advice touted by another. She may take comfort in a book read on Saturday evening, but on Sunday morning she must face a church where change is slow in coming.

I am not proposing a catalyst for theological consensus. Neither am I attempting to persuade the reader that this book contains the final word on any issue confronting women. Instead, I want to change the focus—to direct attention to the choices women must make in the absence of a final word . . . choices that reflect personal responsibility in individual situations.

The guidelines offered here are not intended to minimize the need for change. I applaud those who work for change (particularly those with whom I agree!). But I believe a new perspective is needed if women are to find immediate answers to personal problems.

Many books are written to effect change. Probably an equal number may be found in which the authors attempt to undo change. Once in awhile there arises a need for a book in which we take a look at what to do in the event that change does not come.

This is such a book.

PART 1

THE PROBLEMS AND CHALLENGES FACING WOMEN TODAY

1

THE FRUSTRATIONS OF BEING FEMALE

My friend and I were so engrossed in our last-minute conversation on the drive to the airport that we missed an exit—and I almost missed my flight home. Once aboard, I settled down to continue serious thinking about the events of the trip.

My itinerary had taken me to a variety of speaking engagements in two major cities. The women I spoke with had raised the same questions and issues I had confronted in other places at other times. But this time they left me strangely unsettled.

I needed time to analyze the emerging picture. More and more I saw women searching for biblical answers to issues for which there is no theological consensus—roles, rights, gender restrictions, spiritual gifts, submission. What's a woman to do?

I sensed a restless urgency in some, a defensive determination in others. Mostly I saw frustration and an accelerating search for personhood. By the time we circled for landing in San Francisco, I was beginning to question what I could do. Did the answers lie in a better understanding of personhood? A better understanding of the issues? A change of perspective?

Personhood Often Elusive

A woman is—by definition—a "female person." The gender distinction doesn't connote gender restriction. But though a dictionary can define personhood, it cannot guarantee the privileges of personhood. That responsibility is left to society. And for a woman, personhood is often elusive.

For hundreds of years there have been people who sought to establish the rights of personhood for women. Individually and collectively they fought to promote equality among men and women in the areas of education and career opportunities. Many women are convinced that the rights of personhood will be realized only when all gender lines are erased.

We are seeing dramatic advancements as women assume various roles once occupied exclusively by men. Women climb the corporate ladder. They journey into space. They even make their bid for the White House.

In the religious world seminaries are leading the way. They welcome female students. They endorse female graduates. They seek female faculty members. One mainline evangelical seminary advertised for a New Testament department head, a position that required teaching at a doctoral level. The copy read, "Preference to women candidates."

Still, personhood is often elusive.

Is That All There Is?

Many women are discovering that their achievements are accompanied by a noticeable lack of affirmation. They have made it to the top, but no one applauds. They are achieving in areas once reserved "for men only"—but they often ask, "Is it enough?" These women have found that exercising rights of personhood is not always synonymous with gaining recognition as persons, nor does it necessarily result in fulfillment.

Fulfillment means "to fulfill oneself, to realize completely one's ambitions, potentialities, etc." In other words, fulfillment is simply to have done all you mean (or are meant) to do. Set goals. Reach for them. Achieve. Realize fulfillment.

Reaching goals is tangible. A sense of fulfillment, on the other hand, is less tangible. That's why many people ask, "If this is such a big achievement, why don't I feel fulfilled?" The question "Is that all there is?" may be faced by men and women alike; but it is particularly unsettling to women who have made it through many hurdles and then face the question in the invaded domain at the top.

The Unique Struggles of Christian Women

Christian women have joined the search for personhood as well.

Ideally, a Christian woman may seek to "be" and to "do" just as freely as a "male person"—with no more (and no fewer) restrictions. But just like our peers in the secular world, we face certain obstacles in the pursuit of such privileges.

Problems and Challenges

A woman may overcome many obstacles in order to make it to the top in the religious world, but if her achievements go unrecognized, she feels her personhood is questioned. When one female seminary professor I know was awarded her doctorate, one of her male colleagues asked, "You don't really want us to call you doctor, do you?"

While lack of fulfillment or affirmation is common to both non-Christian and Christian women, the Christian woman faces unique questions regarding gender lines.

"Does being female affect my role as a believer?"

"Does conversion erase gender lines? Reinforce them? Transcend them?"

"Is intelligence a blessing or a curse for a female?"

"Can a woman with nontraditional skills find meaningful ministry within the church body?"

"Am I to be *totally* submissive to my husband?"

The questions are still being debated.

Some churches have ordained women in a drastic attempt to diminish gender lines. Others are still reluctant to use women anywhere other than the church kitchen. The gap between extremes continues to grow.

The current debate over submission further complicates the issue of gender lines and personhood. Through a chain of reactions, the principle of submission has evolved as the focal point of disagreement between two extremes. On the one extreme are those who reject all allusions to a submissive female role. They emphasize that in Christ there is neither male nor female. On the other extreme are those who have adopted submission as the overriding principle. They emphasize that a woman is to obey her husband—no exceptions.

One group sacrifices the *relationship* of marriage as it encourages women to pursue their rights of personhood. The other sacrifices the personhood of the wife as women are advised to preserve the *institution* of marriage at all costs. Essentially it equates passivity with submission.

I do not believe either of these views can be supported. Titus 2:3-5 was the subject of my first book.[1] It was specifically addressed to women with Christian spouses, with no major conflicts. I've always held that the Scriptures teach women to be in submission to their husbands, but I have never believed the principle of submission should override every other principle in the Scriptures. For that matter, I don't believe it's ever biblically correct to emphasize one principle to the exclusion of all others. Whenever any biblical principle is always given precedence over all others, there is potential for serious problems.

Some women have become so intent on submission that they have lost all sense of responsibility. In their confusion, these women deliberately squelch personal spiritual growth so as not to "grow ahead of my husband." Others struggle with the conflict between conscience and submission. Many women choose to go against their consciences because they are convinced it is worse to disobey one's husband than to disobey one's conscience.

In his article "Wife Abuse: The Silent Crime, the Silent Church," Ken Peterson observes that "at least one preacher has said that if a man asks his wife to commit an act of prostitution, she is to submit to his demand."[2]

For years submission has been the subject of heated, highly theoretical discussions among the clergy and seminary students. But today this has become a live issue couched in much confusion and not a little tragedy.

I have counseled with women across the country who have been caught in bizarre situations relating to the issue of submission—wife swapping, accepting a mistress, frequenting nude beaches, spousal abuse. In one case a mother stood by for three years while her spouse sexually molested their young daughter. The tragedy in these cases is twofold. In every case the husband was a professing Christian. (Three were extremely active in the church.) In each case the wife's passivity was reinforced by a spiritual counselor who knew the details of the situation.

It is sobering to realize that problems within the Christian community appear to be no different from problems in the secular world.

This in itself is tragic.

Moreover, we've failed to see that for the Christian woman, these problems are complicated by the added dimension of personal conviction—her own or that of her church body. The battered Christian wife has a restricted course of action. She does not simply ask, "What can I do about spousal abuse?" She must ask, "Do I, as a Christian, have the right to protect myself at the expense of my marriage?"

Lack of Theological Consensus

The theological world is not likely to come to an early consensus on submission, the place of women in the church, or on divorce and remarriage. Not only do Denomination A and Denomination B disagree, but within the ranks of Denomination A policies regarding women vary greatly from congregation to congregation. Seminary professors from the same institution produce books on a common issue with opposing viewpoints. While this says a great deal for academic freedom, it does not say much for theological consensus.

Admittedly the lack of agreement is partly caused by policies which are sometimes based on tradition rather than on close interpretation of Scripture. Numerous books have been written in an attempt to separate truth from tradition. But women with limited theological background are left to wonder where tradition ends and truth begins as one book generates another and one conclusion calls for an opposite.

Focusing on Personal Responsibility

In the midst of this confusion, what course should a woman take?

Concentrate on corporate (female) rights by defying the denomination?

Passively accept something she disagrees with?

Wait for the church to solve the problem by consensus?

None of these choices show personal responsibility. The

first often brings loss of perspective. A sense of responsibility to others disappears in transition. Consumed with the desire to make everything right at the corporate level, a woman often fails to resolve things at a personal level. In the second choice, a woman's very survival may be threatened if she believes she is spiritually obligated to submit under any circumstances. As for the third choice, it seems unrealistic to expect theological consensus over issues so highly debated.

The responsible woman makes choices from a different perspective. She may try to effect change at the corporate level, but she will not lose sight of relationship responsibilities in the process. She may recognize that the lack of theological consensus adds to her problem, but she will not throw up her hands and declare, "This is my problem and it's time for the church to solve it." She will have both the desire and the resources to assume personal responsibility for personal problems.

By assuming responsibility for our own spiritual growth, we build our resources. One of the fundamental errors in current role perception within the Christian community is that a woman's personal relationship with Christ is subjugated to other relationships. Her position is consistently argued "in relationship" . . .

in relationship to her husband,

in relationship to her church,

in relationship to male authority figures in her life.

But too often her most basic relationship is obscured. The woman who enters into a relationship with Jesus Christ assumes lifelong responsibility to nurture that relationship. As a result, she assumes responsibility not only for spiritual growth, but also for her conscience.

While these responsibilities may appear basic, they are, in fact, being laid aside through prolonged attention to "proper role perception," especially through the continued debate over submission.

Dorothy Pape has stated that *role* is not a biblical term. What this means for women, she says, is that "rather than blindly following customs and traditions, each needs to receive personal operational instructions from Christ Himself, plus His power to perform them."[3]

The moment we become new creatures, we are responsible to operate as such. The Scriptures tell us, "If any (wo)man be in Christ (s)he is a new creature. Old things are passed away, behold all things are become new" (2 Corinthians 5:17 KJV). Pursuing personhood will not lead today's Christian woman to answers for complicated questions. She will instead find answers from a better understanding of the responsibilities of New Creaturehood. When a woman becomes a new creature in Christ, there are certain responsibilities imposed upon her which are never diminished—not by circumstances, not by marital status, not by gender lines.

To enable the reader to discover those responsibilities is the goal of this book.

1. Joy Gage, *But You Don't Know Harry* (Wheaton, Illinois: Tyndale, 1972).
2. Kenneth W. Peterson, "Wife Abuse: The Silent Crime, the Silent Church," in *Christianity Today*, November 25, 1983, pp. 22-26.
3. Dorothy Pape, *God and Woman* (Oxford: A. R. Mowbry & Co.; British edition of *In Search of God's Ideal Woman*, first published by InterVarsity Press, 1976), p.14.

PART 2

CHOICES CLARIFIED THROUGH UNDERSTANDING ACCOUNTABILITY

2

IF ANY (WO)MAN BE IN CHRIST

My old college scrapbook contains a bit of history in the making. A newspaper clipping, dateline Los Angeles, reports that after eight weeks and three thousand conversions, "the revival at the Washington and Hill St. tent is closing." (My dormitory was nearby and, along with other students, I had participated in the revival choir on several nights.)

A related clipping includes a photo of three people: the young evangelist, a handsome musician mistakenly identified as Cliff Brown, and a well-known singing cowboy who "hit the sawdust trail" in the canvas cathedral. According to the clipping, "nearly a quarter million people packed the tent during the first five weeks of the city-wide non-denomination revival."

On November 7, 1983—Billy Graham's 65th birthday—a plaque was unveiled at the site of the tent in which he had preached more than three decades earlier. Sponsored jointly by the city and county of Los Angeles, the plaque includes an inscription noting that Graham has preached the gospel in more than sixty countries and to more people than any other man in history.[1]

My last college yearbook includes a picture of a "T. McCully" whom the world now remembers as Ed McCully, one of five martyred missionaries to the Auca Indians. The gospel penetration of Aucaland since the death of McCully and his companions is one of the great missionary stories of this century.

Ed's picture is a sober reminder that instruments (and the way God uses them) may vary, but the catalyst that changes lives is the same. It is the same Lord who causes the Hollywood star to get rid of his race horses and the Auca warrior to lay down his spear. Singing cowboys and spearing savages bear witness that men and women become new creatures through the cross of Christ. Millions of lives have been changed, turned around, redirected because of its catalytic power.

No One Makes the Decision for You

This new identity can never be realized apart from the initiative of the individual. It is here, at the point of conversion, that spiritual accountability begins. No one can make that decision for you:

Not friend.

Not parent.

Not spouse.

The Scriptures clearly teach that every individual will be held accountable for how he responds to Jesus Christ. From the outset spiritual accountability involves a willingness to stand alone, to act when no one else acts, to make a choice when all others procrastinate.

One Lone Woman

In the biblical roster of those who exemplified such accountability, one woman stands out. She was a woman of questionable reputation. Rahab, we are plainly told, was a harlot.

She lived on the Jericho wall in a flatroofed house covered with drying flax. One day two Israelite men came to her home looking for a place to hide. When the king of Jericho demanded that Rahab produce the strangers who had come to spy out the land, she refused. She hid the spies under the flax and sent the king's men on a blind chase. Later the Israelites escaped over the wall by means of a rope hanging from Rahab's window.

Every major Sunday school curriculum includes the story of Rahab the harlot and how she was rewarded for her kindness to the spies. But somewhere in the details learned from early childhood, we miss the profound lesson of a woman's decision to be accountable to God.

We see Rahab's plea for protection but miss her pointed confession of faith (Joshua 2:8-11). We fail to note that in a city where all citizens knew certain facts, one lone woman chose to act upon those facts.

All Jericho had heard about Israel's God of miracles. Had he not dried up the Red Sea? Had he not defeated the kings of the Amorites?

Jericho knew. And Jericho was terrified. Rahab knew. And she confessed to terror such as that of her fellow citizens. But she also confessed what Jericho refused to acknowledge: Israel's God was the true God.

Having acknowledged this to the spies, Rahab pleaded for protection for herself and her family. As every Sunday school scholar knows, the Joshua account ends with her family's survival when Jericho's walls tumbled down.

But Rahab's story does not end there. The confrontation with the spies became more than a mutually advantageous military liaison. It marked the beginning of Rahab's spiritual journey.

Rahab is one of only two women mentioned by name in Hebrews 11. The writer of this great chapter on heroes of faith declares, "By faith the harlot Rahab perished not with them that believed not" (11:31 KJV).

In addition Matthew 1:5 lists Rahab in the genealogy of Jesus. Such were the far-reaching results of one woman's decision to be spiritually accountable.

For the twentieth-century individual spiritual accountability begins with a response to the cross of Christ.

What Applies To Me?

But what does spiritual accountability involve for a woman?

The basic responsibility for all believers is to center everything in life around a personal relationship with God, including obedience to him based on an ongoing study of his word, resulting in a new lifestyle. The apostle Peter reminds those who are "born again" that their lifestyle should no longer include base attitudes or action; instead, we are commanded to long for spiritual food (the word of God) and to grow from it (1 Peter 1:23, 2:1-2).

Peter later enumerates growth goals for the believer:

> Add to your faith goodness;
> and to goodness, knowledge;
> and to knowledge, self-control;

and to self-control, perseverance;
and to perseverance, godliness;
and to godliness, brotherly kindness;
and to brotherly kindness, love.
(2 Peter 1:5-7)

Further, he states that any believer who neglects these goals is blind and has forgotten how he was cleansed from sin (1:9).

I believe we may safely assume that Peter's admonitions, addressed to those of like faith, are intended for women as well as men. The spiritual goals set before all believers are for women as well as men.

Personal Responsibility Obscured

Throughout the evangelical community, women see themselves caught in the conflict over spiritual goals. A woman wanting to develop her relationship with Jesus Christ may hesitate to pursue this goal if her husband is not a growing believer. The message she receives is that "your husband is your spiritual head." But her responsibility toward her spiritual head remains a subject of debate. If a husband demonstrates little interest in spiritual goals, the wife is often unsure what to do spiritually. She feels stymied if her husband does not lead in spiritual matters. Ironically, single women often feel the same because they have no spiritual head.

If not resolved, this conflict can effectively limit a woman's access to spiritual goals. Growth goals are often set aside. Connie, a single employee of a parachurch organization, functions in what she defines as a "spiritual holding pattern." Her best friend is married to a mature believer whose leadership sets the spiritual tone in the home. Connie is convinced she will never experience growth like her friend's until she too is married to such a man.

Women receive spiritual direction through many channels today—the local church, Christian books, Christian radio and television, a favorite tape ministry, or even self-appointed spiritual gurus. By whatever vehicle the messages come, if a woman allows it to define her personal accountability, she will become confused over spiritual goals. It is our responsibility to practice discernment as listeners—to filter the messages received.

"I hear more about *being* a Godly woman than about surviving as a Godly woman," wrote one young friend. "I am told my husband is my spiritual head, but how do I follow his lead when he is spiritually immature?"

She has articulated well the paradoxical nature of the demand. A growing relationship with Jesus Christ is the lifeline of all believers and our most basic spiritual goal. No believer should be required to thwart that growth.

Many women are no longer certain of their responsibility toward obedience to God versus obedience to spouse. Obedience to God is proclaimed the primary responsibility of all believers. But women are often told to set aside this responsibility if and when it conflicts with obedience to one's husband. In their confusion women may set aside obedience goals. If they do, guilt and hostility often follow.

We should question any theory which modifies the individual's responsibility toward God. It is every woman's responsibility to be the best example of a believer she can be. She is to strive to attain to her capacity in knowledge, understanding, and maturity. Any theory which limits such potential is biblically inconsistent.

The responsible woman knows that God demands personal accountability of all believers in matters of growth and obedience. She realizes that if she diminishes accountability (or allows it to be diminished), she is inviting endless frustration. (In the next two chapters I will address more fully the problems that limit growth and obedience.)

WILL MY GROWTH THREATEN MY HUSBAND?

I am sometimes asked, "How would you advise a woman who finds that her spiritual maturity poses a threat to her husband?"

In a recent interview with Dr. Roy Kraft, pastor of Twin Lakes Baptist Church in Aptos, California, I posed that very question. He wisely observed, "True spirituality has, as one of its indications, true humility. We don't force our experience on others."

Dr. Kraft's statement draws our attention to the importance of definition. We must be careful in defining spiritual maturity. The very concept carries with it the idea of relationship skills. However gifted, however talented, however knowledgeable a woman may be, *if she has no relationship skills, she is not demonstrating spiritual maturity.*

We have only to look at Paul's letter to the Corinthians to verify this. The Corinthians were knowledgeable. They were zealous. They were bold about sharing their faith. They possessed many spiritual gifts. They even anticipated eagerly the Lord's return from heaven. Yet they were not mature believers, as was illustrated by their lack of people skills. They demonstrated no love or compassion. They were proud. They were devisive.[2]

In 1 Corinthians 13 Paul emphasizes that gifts and knowledge are ineffective except within the context of love. The spiritually mature woman recognizes this. Her maturity is most evident in the way she handles relationships, including her relationship with her husband.

It's often easier to recognize that your spouse feels threatened than it is to determine the underlying cause. It's easier to accept the obvious explanation than to discover the real cause.

While I was working on this chapter, I asked my husband, "In what way did you feel threatened by me in the early years of our marriage?"

"You knew more about ministry than I did," he replied without a moment's hesitation. Then he added, "It wasn't just that you had an opinion on everything, it was that you were so opinionated."

The truth is, I did know more about the inner workings of a local church than he did (which is not to say I knew much about "ministry"). Ken received his early spiritual training in a nontraditional church setting, from a pastor he has always regarded as his spiritual mentor. Though Ken received excellent teaching, nothing in the experience prepared him to function in an organized church.

By contrast, I grew up in a more typical church setting, and even worked as a church secretary—a great way of learning a church's inner workings. I also served as a missionary under a home missions board. I came into our marriage thinking, *I'm going to be such a big help. I have this diploma in Christian Education and all this valuable experience.* But I soon discovered Ken didn't want me messing in his Christian Education program. I sensed that he felt threatened by my wonderful credentials, and I was devastated.

My lack of people skills—not my credentials—made Ken feel threatened. I was oblivious to the insecurity he felt as a first-time pastor three months out of Bible college. Instead I quickly voiced my opinion on everything—demonstrating, I felt, my ability to think. I was amazed to discover that Ken thought this meant I wanted to control his decisions.

It took time, but eventually I learned it wasn't necessary to always express my opinion. I also discovered that relationships flourish best between people who know how and when to express personal opinions.

If a woman believes her husband feels threatened by her spiritual maturity, she should ask herself, "Is anything else contributing to the problem?" Advanced education, family background, or a stronger personality are only a few of the factors that could feasibly threaten one's spouse. But such hurdles can be overcome with commitment, time, and patience.

I recall a couple from one of our churches who had been married more than thirty years. The husband was a hard-working, self-employed man who had never completed elementary school. The wife had earned a master's degree, and now kept the family's books. The mutual respect they held for one another was obvious. I don't know all that went into making that marriage work, but I believe I discovered one important clue: In all the time we knew them she never so much as raised an eyebrow (much less corrected him) when he "murdered the King's English." She saw the pluses in his life and refused to linger on the minuses. In spite of her advanced education, he had no reason to feel threatened.

I'm not sure there's a simple solution when a man feels threatened by his wife. But I'm quite sure that true growth never results in flaunting knowledge, gifts, or skills. Certainly it doesn't result in a one-woman campaign to change a husband. And forgoing personal growth is never the answer.

Focusing on Personal Responsibility

The threat to a spouse is not the only reason women choose not to grow spiritually. As we will see in the following chapter, some women ignore their responsibility for personal growth out of a misinterpretation of spiritual headship. For whatever reason, it is error just the same.

We need the spiritual resources that accompany spiritual maturity. The greater our problems, the more we need the resources. True spiritual growth is always an asset—never a liability. To pursue that growth is not only our right, but also our responsibility.

1. Russell Chandler, "Los Angeles Honors Billy Graham," in *Christianity Today*, December 16, 1983, pp. 34-35.

2. This subject is examined in the book *Restoring Fellowship, Judgment, and Church Discipline* by Ken and Joy Gage (Chicago: Moody Press, 1984).

3

SPIRITUAL HEADSHIP: THE MYTH AND THE REALITY

On the bench beside me, Bobbie squirmed. Soon her squirming turned to muttering. *She's fuming,* I thought. *If this speaker opens the session to questions, she'll explode.*

"Come on, Bobbie, let's talk," I suggested when the seminar was over, and I steered her outside beneath the pines. As we settled on a fallen log, I encouraged her to tell me what was gnawing at her.

"What good does it do to draw me a chart of how things are supposed to be?" she demanded. "Why don't they ever tell me how to make it work?" For thirty minutes she poured out her frustrations over her fifteen-year failure to understand what spiritual headship is all about. Her husband, a believer for many years, made unwise decisions (and doesn't everyone at one time or another?) which she never questioned because she felt it would be tantamount to questioning his headship. His failure to consistently read and discuss the Bible with her was disillusioning. Bobbie had a great capacity for understanding Scripture, but without her husband's prompting she never felt the freedom to pursue a concentrated course of Bible study.

In part Bobbie's problem stemmed from overexposure to seminars which expound a system but give no suggestions about what to do when the system breaks down. It also stemmed from her misinterpretation of spiritual headship.

Without quite understanding what happened, Bobbie placed primary responsibility for her spiritual growth on her husband, because that's how she perceived his role as her spiritual head. In the process she forced herself into a position of limited spiritual accountability: If her husband failed his God-given duty, Bobbie might shrivel up—but he would be to blame.

The Mythical Ultimate Resource

A woman's perception of God's order can cloud her perception of spiritual accountability.

I have observed that many women link their lack of growth to deficient spiritual headship. Their belief is the byproduct of a myth.

According to The Myth, spiritual headship means being the ultimate or primary resource for spiritual growth. As such, the husband must assume responsibility for his wife's spiritual growth. Just how much responsibility that leaves her is not quite clear, but it is considerably less then that of her unmarried peers or of women married to unbelievers. These women also have their myths. The unmarried and those married to unbelievers believe that "When I have a husband . . ." or "When my husband becomes a Christian. . ."

Women don't always articulate this ideal. But when questioned less overtly, they frequently allude to the tension between reality and the ideal. They may readily assent to personal responsibility, but they also communicate that lurking in the back of their minds is the idea that God's ideal structure begins with a husband who is the Ultimate Resource for spiritual growth. Outside that structure they feel handicapped and discouraged—"How can I be expected to reach a level of maturity when I have no one to encourage or lead me spiritually?"

The woman who holds to The Myth unwittingly shifts spiritual accountability. In her mind the husband becomes responsible for his wife's growth, and she in turn assumes the unwelcome responsibility for ensuring that he performs as expected. She's constrained to concentrate on her husband's growth because without it, she feels doomed to a zero growth rate. She concentrates on manipulating her husband into a leadership role, and puts her own growth goals "on hold."

The woman who does not swallow The Myth assumes responsibility for her own growth.

My own spiritual growth has profited from a husband who definitely has the gift of teaching. He has, in fact, given me the keys for spiritual development. He taught me how to study, and convinced me I could (and should) dig for deeper truths on my own. But what if he had not discipled me? What if he had been a businessman with little talent for teaching? Would that have detracted from his headship?

No, I don't think so.

Somewhere along the line, the basic meaning of headship

has been buried beneath unrealistic expectations spawned by The Myth.

Never is a woman's faulty perception of headship more evident than when she raises the issue of "family devotions." Frequently I am asked, "How does your husband handle devotions?" Somehow the question always sounds more like an indictment. The tone of voice communicates, "My husband is a miserable failure in this department, and I want you to tell me how to shape him up."

In many cases the husband in question is a dedicated Christian. He may even believe that couples should have this daily sharing time, but for one reason or another, he fails to initiate it. He might respond to a little prompting—but that's against the rules. The Myth says that prompting a husband diminishes his headship, so wives must never prompt. The truth is, prompting is permissible; but nagging is a no-no.

If a shared time in God's word is important to a wife, then she should express her desire. It's simple enough to say, "Dear, it would mean a lot to me if we could spend a few minutes together reading the Bible and praying for our home." If he doesn't respond positively, she shouldn't insist. She should, instead, concentrate on her own private reading and prayer.

It took years of patience and one well-chosen moment of prompting to persuade my father to pray aloud. My parents had been believers for a number of years but my mother's spiritual growth had progressed more rapidly than her husband's. Daily she spent time reading the Bible and praying in the privacy of her room. At mealtime they always paused for prayer but it was Mother's duty to pray, three meals each day, 365 days a year.

Then one day, instead of praying, Mother made a short speech. "I don't think I should be the only one to thank God for our food. Today is my birthday, and I think you should pray."

"You're absolutely right," Father agreed. And that was the beginning of his praying aloud.

While the incident was a significant step in my father's growth, it has less to do with his position in the home than The

Myth would have us believe. He had met the qualifications outlined in Ephesians for years. He certainly demonstrated love to his wife and none of us ever doubted that he considered it his responsibility to protect her and his family. His headship was not determined by his ability to pray aloud, to instruct his wife, or to display natural abilities of leadership.

Spiritual Headship: Documented Version

According to Ephesians 5:23-33, a man is to love his wife as much as his own self, and enough to die for her if necessary. He is to leave father and mother for her, and to care for her and provide for her. Clearly this speaks of a relationship between two people. When a man is a loving, caring, sacrifical husband, he meets the qualifications of headship whether or not he excels as a leader or a student. The relationship parallels that of Christ and the church, as Elisabeth Elliot observes: "Christ laid down his life for his bride, the church. There is no 'bossism,' no tyranny, no cruelty in his being our head. So the husband is to love his wife and take responsibility for her, to care for her, provide for her, lay down his life for her, make her holy."[1]

On the same passage in Ephesians 5, Beverly LaHaye comments, "Husbands are told to love their wives, just as Christ loved the church: Christ's love for the church was sacrificial, even to the point of giving himself up for her! When this kind of love and submission exists between husband and wife, then the matter of headship or authority does not become a divisive issue."[2]

However, headship or authority does become a divisive issue when Ephesians 5 is seen as a command manual rather than a relationship model. I'll address problems arising as a result of this error in chapter four, but for now I want to dispel the myth that spiritual headship is contingent upon natural leadership ability.

Turning Husbands into Spiritual Giants

If propelled by The Myth, a woman will attempt to force or manipulate her husband into a position of spiritual leadership.

Sincere and well-meaning, but frustrated and ineffective, this woman assumes a terrible burden of responsibility for her husband's role. It is not enough to acknowledge his authority. She feels she must somehow find a way to help him become the leader she thinks a spiritual head ought to be. This sometimes leads to deliberate inhibiting of growth. With something akin to paranoia she exclaims, "But I don't want to grow ahead of my husband!"

We cannot make spiritual giants of men by choosing to be spiritual dwarfs ourselves. We can neither force nor manipulate men into positions of leadership.

Only the ministry of the Holy Spirit can accomplish this type of growth. When a woman assumes the responsibility of doing the work of the Holy Spirit, she assumes responsibility for something far beyond her control. This invariably leads to only one thing—high-level frustration.

I'm certainly not saying that men have no responsibility toward the spiritual growth of their families. I'm saying that any problems, real or imagined, perpetrated by spiritually deficient husbands cannot be resolved solely by their wives.

Teaching which should be directed to men is instead often offered in a seminar for women. This sometimes heightens the frustration. As a woman writing to women, I have no editorial responsibility to define a man's responsibility. That must come in books directed to men and from the pulpits of our churches. My purpose is to encourage women to be spiritually responsible, whatever their circumstances.

I encourage you to by all means pray for your husband. Expect God to mold him. Let the Holy Spirit do his work. And finally, pray for the special discernment and wisdom needed to focus on the positive. The responsible woman will not diminish a man who is a loving, protective provider because he is naturally inept in communicating spiritual things.

Spiritual Giants: Female Gender

The very mention of spiritual growth always brings to my mind two women, both spiritual giants. One has never married, the other married at age 42. Each made an impact on my life because of her deep personal walk with the Lord, developed without benefit of the mythical Ultimate Resource.

Fern, who stayed single, was my mentor as well as my friend. We met right after I finished Bible college. She had already spent more than a dozen years in an isolated section of the Ozark Mountains teaching the Bible to hundreds of people. She held a master's degree from the University of Iowa, but regretted that she never had the opportunity to attend Bible college.

She was not, however, without resources and creativity.

Fern attended seminary on her couch. Well-prepared by her education to be an independent scholar, she could study the Scriptures on her own.

Fern also realized her radio could do much more than keep her company while she did housework. Through radio Bible programs she had access to solid teaching that could enhance her personal study. She requested by mail the study outlines offered on the programs, and with notes and Bible in hand, went to class on her living room sofa for several hours every week.

My other friend was a forty-two-year-old bride when I met her. Her attitudes revealed the depth of her spiritual maturity, and her speech showed the depth of her biblical knowledge. Since she was a new bride, I knew her maturity and knowledge developed without benefit of the mythical Ultimate Resource. She has one continuous challenge for women who want to grow: Get into God's word and study it. Then get into his word and study more. It is hard to improve on that advice. Certainly with the abundance of material available for independent study today, women are without excuse.

Though many women have challenged me by their lives, none have challenged me more than some of those married to unbelievers. They face unique problems. Not only do they lack encouragement, they are often forbidden to get involved in the Christian community. Sunday morning worship may be the only church meeting they can attend. Opportunities for ministry are usually limited.

I think of Cindy. Because her husband strenuously objected to any church participation beyond Sunday morning, we rarely saw her during the week. But she had a growing relationship with God as evidenced by her life—proof that "going" and "growing" are not synonymous. An eager student, she studied on her own, took advantage of home study courses, and was better versed in the Scriptures than most people in her church.

Growth in the Face of Opposition

For some women, growing spiritually will continue to be a lonely journey with little encouragement or outlet. If you find yourself in this category, I encourage you to consider the life of one of Jesus' closest followers, Mary of Bethany.

Some scholars believe Mary had greater spiritual perception than any other follower of Jesus during his life on earth.[3] But she had limited opportunity to demonstrate that perception; at times she faced opposition, both from family and from other disciples.

The twelve apostles, who followed Jesus constantly, were for the most part opportunistic, slow to learn, and generally obtuse in spiritual matters. They had their best moments: John basked in Jesus' presence and came to be known as the beloved disciple; Andrew was quick to bring others to the Messiah; and Peter, who would later so grievously deny Jesus, at one time had faith enough to walk on water (for a short distance only). And yet, although all twelve were present on three occasions when their Master said he would die and be raised from the dead, none comprehended the statement. None gave evidence at the time of any lasting spiritual perception.

And one betrayed him.

In the post-resurrection years, Peter and John, together with Paul, became the church's great teachers. Transformed by the Holy Spirit, they were spiritual giants who carried on God's plan. Today we turn to their divinely inspired writings, knowing that God's word is our Ultimate Resource for spiritual growth.

But Mary of Bethany didn't have equal opportunity to hear the Master because she wasn't with him every day as the Twelve were. She never had opportunity to walk on water, cut off an enemy's ear, watch with Jesus in agonizing prayer, or acknowledge her allegiance to him around a courtyard fire. She didn't see his transfiguration, but when she sat at Jesus' feet with dozens of others, she paid close attention to his words. She comprehended what he said and responded accordingly. What she learned affected her actions before and after his death.

With costly perfume Mary silently anointed Jesus before the eyes of the disciples. She was criticized for her gesture, just as she had been criticized for sitting at his feet. Her act of anointing Christ should have spoken dramatically to the disciples. Even when Jesus explained to them that she did it for his burial, the message of the act escaped them. They were critical of the cost, of the woman, of the waste. Her act of worship had little effect on them.

Mary of Bethany is not listed among the women who went to the tomb. Some scholars interpret this as evidence that she wasn't there—that she refused to go.[4] The women were intent on embalming the body if they found someone to roll away the stone. But Mary knew it would be a pointless pilgrimage—Jesus wouldn't be at the tomb. She stayed away because of her spiritual understanding.

Focusing on Personal Responsibility

In whatever situation she finds herself, the responsible Christian woman should seize every opportunity to grow spiritually. Whether married or single, she will assume responsibility for her own growth because she recognizes that the true ultimate resource is Jesus Christ and his word.

1. "Christian Leaders Respond," in *Today's Christian Woman*, March/April, 1984, pp. 57-59.
2. Also from "Christian Leaders Respond."
3. *The Scofield Bible*, p. 1090, note 1: "Mary alone of the disciples understood Christ's repeated declaration concerning His own death and resurrection (John 12:3-7). Save Mary, not one of the disciples but Peter, and he only in the great confession (Matthew 16:16), manifested a spark of spiritual intelligence till after the resurrection of Christ and the impartation of the Spirit (John 20:22; Acts 2:1-4).
4. *The Scofield Bible*, p. 1037, note 1: "But Mary of Bethany, who alone of our Lord's disciples had comprehended His thrice repeated announcement of His coming death and resurrection, invested the anointing with deeper meaning of the preparation of His body for burying. Mary of Bethany was not among the women who went to the sepulcher with intent to embalm the body of Jesus."

4

MY CONSCIENCE, MY RESPONSIBILITY

I had just expressed to a young missionary my joy over a recent event in our church: Despite severe opposition from her husband, a spiritually sensitive Hispanic woman had made an important step in her Christian life. On her own, without urging from anyone other than the Holy Spirit, she had concluded that her continued obedience to the Lord required her identification with him through baptism. The night of her baptism was a thrilling occasion.

As I recounted these details, I watched expectantly for the missionary's delight. Instead, to my surprise and dismay, he declared that the woman had made a bad choice: "She should have been submissive to her husband."

How different is this attitude from that of early Christians who laid down their lives because of their convictions! In *Church History in Plain Language*, Bruce Shelley shows how early believers in the midst of a politically hostile environment remained faithful followers of the God who invaded time. Shelley describes the emergence of Christianity from its Jewish roots. It was this separation from Judaism that brought about persecution by Rome. Once the Christians could no longer be considered just another sect within Judaism, they were persecuted severely. In spite of the persecution, Christianity spread extraordinarily. "Early Christians were moved by a burning conviction," Shelley states. "The Event had happened. God had invaded time and Christians were captivated by the creative power of that grand news."[1]

How easy it would have been to compromise one's conscience in order to survive! How often they were challenged, even ordered, to do just that. Polycarp, for example, was told to simply swear by Caesar. But he declared, "I am a Christian." Refusing to deny his conscience, he went to his burning death. Rather than welcome the protection of a political system that denied his doctrine, he welcomed the flames.

Centuries later an Indian prince made a similarly hard choice. His decision to follow Christ did not cost his life but it cost him everything else, including his family. His obedience to his conscience inspired the popular chorus, "I Have Decided to Follow Jesus." I remember the thrill of those lyrics as I joined the voices of four thousand young people as we declared our unified intention to do no less than the Indian prince.

My conversation with the missionary took place ten years ago. Since that time I have spoken to many who espouse this brand of submission. And I have wondered about the road evangelicals have traveled between the Indian prince and the Hispanic housewife. For centuries we have held as heroes those who stood for their beliefs, who refused to deny their conscience. But now, that which once thrilled us has become suspect. It is no longer acceptable in all evangelical circles to follow one's convictions if it means disobedience to one's spouse. I was more than a little disturbed the first time I confronted this thinking. Somewhere, something of value has been lost.

Passivity: Once No Virtue, Now *The* Virtue

We have only to look at our roots to see that passivity in the face of moral choices has never been considered a virtue among believers. Today, that which was never a virtue has become The Virtue.

I was cornered at a woman's conference by an avid supporter of The Virtue. Her comments, entirely unrelated to my keynote address, were at first random, then turned abruptly to a woman's responsibility to be submissive. She recalled in great detail several incidents from her "counseling ministry." Although she indicated that she was not a trained counselor, the cases she recounted were complicated. Her "solution," on the other hand, could be summarized in one sentence, "When women submit to their husbands, God will take care of the problems."

I questioned her about specific problems. "What should a Christian woman do if her husband beats her?"

"If a woman is being beaten, she's asking for it."

"Suppose it's a child who is being beaten?" I prodded. "Suppose the husband sexually abuses a daughter?" Before she answered, I assured her my interest was not entirely theoretical: "I have personal knowledge of Christian couples in these situations."

She nodded. Through lips which appeared to be permanently tightened, she replied, "I still believe a woman has to honor the Lord by maintaining her place of submission. She should just pray and let the Lord take care of everything."

In one glib statement she managed to relieve a woman of legal responsibility, moral responsibility, and maternal responsibility—all under the guise of spiritual responsibility.

Of all the dangerous theories foisted on women today, the most personally damaging is perpetrated by those who equate biblical submission with passivity. This view of submission states that obedience to one's husband must always take precedence over obedience to one's conscience.

Making Evil Good

Many women are caught in the conflict between conscience and submission. Ironically, their dilemma comes from a sincere attempt to be spiritually responsible. These women don't willingly condone evil, but their role, as they perceive it, leaves them without choice. It forces them to label "good" what they know to be evil.

One troubled wife pleaded for advice because her husband has an insatiable desire for pornographic material. "Sometimes he insists that I go see 'slicks' with him," she said. "I know I'm supposed to submit to my husband, but I feel so torn."

Women who have been convinced that passivity is the only acceptable definition of biblical submission often feel torn. If a woman continues to view submission from the perspective of her relationship to her husband—if the issue is seen purely as to submit or not to submit—her dilemma might never be solved.[2]

If we are to resolve the question of submission versus conscience, we must address it from the perspective of a woman's relationship to God. This relationship demands moral responsibility. Until we acknowledge that a woman is morally responsible to God, the debate over passive submission is just so many words. Once this responsibility is acknowledged, however, moral choices become clear—but not necessarily easy.

NELDA'S CHOICE

Nelda is one woman who, in spite of bad counsel, made a responsible choice. Her husband was extremely active in their church. In fact, he was known as the pastor's right-hand man. Then, after eighteen years of marriage, he had an affair with another woman. He asked Nelda for a divorce, saying he was in love with the other woman.

Nelda was wondering how she would face the future with thirteen-year-old twins to support, when another blow fell. Her husband decided he didn't want a divorce after all. He loved both women and he wanted to stay married to Nelda and continue to see his lover.

Nelda refused to reconcile on those terms and told her husband she did not feel such an arrangement could be honoring to the Lord.

Then the third blow fell. Their pastor came to call. He had been told that Nelda's husband wanted to reconcile and he proposed that Nelda submit to his terms. Not believing the pastor understood the arrangement correctly, Nelda explained the terms of the reconciliation. "I don't believe God would have me be part of such an arrangement," she declared. Whereupon the pastor counseled her, "As bad as the situation may be, some women would be willing to make that sacrifice in order to avoid a divorce." He thought Nelda should also be willing.

Nelda wasn't.

She refused to consent to the proposed arrangement; her husband filed for a divorce. Nelda was then forced to either confess her sin of divorce or leave her church. She left her church, but not the Lord.

When I met her, Nelda was actively involved in another church. She acknowledged the practical problems imposed upon her by her husband's willfulness. "But I've learned to depend upon the Lord more," she commented, "I know I made the right decision. I had no other choice."

Avoiding Perpetuation of Error

Many sincere Christian women are vulnerable to erroneous teaching. In their desire to grow they gravitate toward a certain speaker or a "spiritual guru" and forget to use discernment. Authority figures tend to command our automatic trust—but sometimes that trust is undeserved.

We must learn to reject any concept requiring us to disobey God's revealed moral law in order to be God's woman. We must not build our obedience to God through a blind following of concepts popularized through the latest seminar. Sometimes, as in Nelda's case, we must even go against the advice of our spiritual mentors.

The biblical Bereans are held before us as an example. These first-century Christians are described as more noble than those in Thessalonica because they searched the Scriptures daily to evaluate the truth of the apostles' message.

> As soon as it was night, the brothers sent Paul and Silas away to Berea. On arriving there, they went to the Jewish synagogue. Now the Bereans were of more noble character than the Thessalonians, for they received the message with great eagerness and examined the Scriptures every day to see if what Paul said was true (Acts 17:10-11).

These verses infer that believers have a responsibility to test teaching.

The process of testing what we are taught involves both sound *interpretation* and sound *theology.* The concept of passive submission is suspect in both areas.

A teaching may be tested *interpretively* in several ways. Theologians make use of language and historical data. This isn't usually possible for those who are less trained, but there is a more basic method of testing teaching which we can all use.

Any believer can make use of the context test. Often, erroneous teachings evolve when a verse or a phrase is lifted from its context and expounded without regard to surrounding passages. This has the same effect as lifting one sentence out of a ten page letter and interpreting the sentence by itself. It's possible that one's interpretation of the single sentence could be inconsistent with the true intent of the writer. No amount of analyzing the sentence will determine its true meaning if the other ten pages are ignored.

In Ephesians 5:22-24, we read:

> Wives, submit to your husbands as to the Lord. For the husband is the head of the wife as Christ is the head of the church, his body, of which he is the Savior. Now as the church submits to Christ, so also wives should submit to their husbands in everything.

Taken by itself, this passage could appear to be the perfect proof text for those who espouse passive submission. The final words "in everything" seem to be particularly supportive of the teaching. Indeed, "in everything" could be interpreted to mean a woman must disobey her conscience, if necessary, in order to obey her husband.

But we have only to read the chapter to discover that a believer is never to partake in immorality. Paul spends half the chapter expounding the moral standard for believers. It is irresponsible to even suggest that this standard should be set aside in an attempt to make one verse, or one phrase, stand alone.

To test teaching *theologically,* we must look for consistency. One doctrine cannot contradict another.

No matter what our definition of biblical submission, God still holds us morally responsible. Many of the concessions women are required to make in the name of passive submission are clearly condemned in the Scriptures. We cannot ignore this contradiction.

For example, 1 Corinthians 5 takes a dim view of incest, even between consenting adults:

> It is actually reported that there is sexual immorality among you, and of a kind that does not occur even among pagans: A man has his father's wife. And you are proud! . . . When you are assembled in the name of our Lord Jesus . . . hand this man over to Satan, so that the sinful nature may be destroyed and his spirit saved on the day of the Lord (1-4).

So serious is this sin that Paul demanded the offender's immediate expulsion from the body. How much greater the sin when perpetrated by a father upon his minor child. If a mother passively accepts her husband's participation in this despicable crime, won't she also be guilty?

To say that a woman must disobey her conscience or God's revealed moral laws in order to fulfill the biblical requirement of submission is theologically inconsistent. Any concept which requires a woman to make moral concessions in the name of submission is theologically suspect.

SAPPHIRA'S EXAMPLE

The negative example of one New Testament woman sheds light on the question of conscience. Acts 5 records the case of Ananias and Sapphira, a husband and wife who were part of the fellowship of believers at Jerusalem.

Ananias was not such a bad sort if one measures him by human standards. We have no reason to believe he beat his wife or his children, if indeed there were children. Nothing in the record indicates that he was a womanizer. What he asked his wife to do pales in comparison to current spousal demands supported by the passive-submission crowd.

Ananias had just one problem: a great need to be recognized. He wanted to be Mr. Nice Guy, a front-runner for the "Most Benevolent Man of the Year" award. He wanted to be lauded as good and generous.

But he wanted to accomplish all this without personal sacrifice.

In time he devised a plan to sell an expendable piece of

property, give part of the money to the church and tell them he was donating all of it. Then he, like Barnabas, would be hailed for his great generosity.

His wife agreed to support his plan. Ananias sold his property, made his contribution, lied to the apostles, and was struck dead by the Holy Spirit.

Three hours later Sapphira ambled in, oblivous to the her husband's recent demise. The apostles questioned her, giving her one last opportunity to show that someone in the family had a conscience. She was given a choice—support her husband's lie or tell the truth. She lied, just as Ananias did. And she died, just as Ananias did.

Sapphira was held accountable for her complicity in her husband's deception.

In *God and Women* Dorothy Pape takes note of Sapphira's part in her husband's scheme. "We are given no clue about which of the women in Acts is God's ideal," Pape declares, "but we can be reasonably sure it was not Sapphira." According to Pape, "when it comes to a moral issue, a woman cannot be blindly obedient to a husband and shelter under the 'weaker sex' label. We must face the solemn fact that . . . God requires the same high moral standard from every disciple, man or woman."[3]

Is God Concerned about the Conscience?

God's concern about the conscience is quite evident in the Scriptures. Paul could tell the Sanhedrin, "My brothers, I have fulfilled my duty to God in all good conscience to this day" (Acts 23:1). In a later appearance before his accusers, he added, "I strive always to keep my conscience clear before God and man" (Acts 24:16).

Peter wrote,

> Always be prepared to give an answer to everyone who asks you to give the reason for the hope that you have. But do this with gentleness and respect, keeping a clear conscience (1 Peter 3:15-16).

In Hebrews 9:14, after a look at Old Testament ceremonial sacrifices, we are reminded,

> How much more, then, will the blood of Christ, who through the eternal Spirit offered himself unblemished to God, cleanse our consciences from acts that lead to death, so that we may serve the living God!

Legitimate questions regarding a good conscience frequently arise: "How can I know my conscience is sensitive enough?" or "Is it possible my conscience is too sensitive?"

One way the conscience is sensitized is through God's word. If one doesn't know what the Bible says on certain moral matters, it's entirely possible to have an underdeveloped conscience. Fifteen years ago, an eighteen-year-old single girl came to my husband for counseling. She was a new believer and had no prior exposure to biblical teaching. At one point in their session she interrupted Ken and asked with disbelief, "Do you mean it's wrong to sleep with your boyfriend? If you really love one another, doesn't that make it all right?"

An underdeveloped conscience doesn't give license to do what seems to be "all right." The word of God takes precedence over the conscience. To develop the conscience, one must be in the Scriptures.

Problems with an oversensitive conscience often arise over issues that are not so specifically covered in Scriptures. We call these "disputable matters." In his letter to the Romans, Paul deals with the oversensitive conscience and disputable matters (Romans 14). He concludes that those with oversensitive consciences should not judge those with fewer convictions. But those with fewer convictions should take care not to offend the oversensitive consciences of fellow believers.[4]

There will be times when a woman must decide if her convictions stem from an oversensitive conscience and, if so, whether a compromise is in order. Many years ago one woman confided in me her struggle with her conscience. She was active in a local church which frowned upon movies of any kind. Her husband, a new believer, enjoyed an occasional movie. "He doesn't ask much," she said, "and he is careful about the movies he chooses. I'd rather not go, but I've decided I should do it for him."

But what if "giving in" doesn't seem to be the right choice? What should a woman do? Ultimately each woman must make her own decision before the Lord. The responsible woman will take advantage of all available resources—books or tapes which address the issue, and counsel from a trusted older friend, pastor, or trained counselor. Above all she should ask God for wisdom, for sensitivity toward her husband, and for needed communication skills. In discussing the problem with her husband she emphasizes her feelings because feelings are less threatening. "Honey, I know you really want me to do this, but when I do it I feel—"

It isn't always easy, but it's always important to move wisely when it comes to matters of conscience.

Focusing on Personal Responsibility

The amount of internal evidence shows that God demands personal responsibility in matters of conscience. This responsibility does not diminish because of gender or marital status.

To be without principles is to be without conscience. It matters little if principles are lost because of politically hostile systems or through erroneous teaching. The end result is the same. To deny the conscience is to forsake principle.

The Scriptures relating to submission are among the most highly debated in evangelical circles today. Much ink is spent in defining submission. The correct interpretation of biblical submission will continue to raise questions, many of which are valid.

It is not so important that we define submission to the satisfaction of all. But it is crucial that we refute the theory which equates moral passivity with biblical submission. It must be denied at all levels within the evangelical community, and by the individuals within that community.

Women may feel powerless to effect change at the top, but every woman can—and must—assume responsibility for her own conscience.

1. Bruce L. Shelley, *Church History in Plain Language* (Waco, Texas: Word Books, 1982), p. 49.

2. Shelley refers to moral decisions confronting first-century female believers: "Unlike his pagan neighbor, the Christian refused to take his weak and unwanted children out in the woods and leave them to die or be picked up by robbers. If a Christian woman was married to a pagan and a girl baby was born, the father might say, 'Throw her out,' but the mother would usually refuse" (p. 55).

3. Dorothy Pape, *God and Women* (Oxford: A. R. Mowbry & Co.; British edition of *In Search of God's Ideal Woman*,first published by InterVarsity Press, 1976), p.76.

4. The matter of the conscience and disputable matters is discussed at length in chapters 9 and 10 of *Restoring Fellowship Judgment and Church Discipline* by Ken and Joy Gage (Chicago: Moody Press, 1984).

PART 3

MAKING RESPONSIBLE CHOICES CONCERNING SPIRITUAL GIFTS

5

SPIRITUAL GIFTS: WHAT'S A WOMAN TO DO?

The subject of spiritual gifts has commanded much attention in recent years. "How to discover your gift" has been a popular theme for books, Bible studies, and sermons. There are even spiritual gift quizzes: Answer a series of questions and presto!—your spiritual gift is identified.

Unfortunately, discovering one's gift does not necessarily lead to exercising it. One woman who tried one of these quizzes commented laughingly, "I flunked hospitality and all those womanly things, but I got a perfect score in teaching and preaching." Currently she belongs to a church that does not allow women to teach above the middle childhood level, but she says she has "no real experience with children."

Circumstances can prevent the exercise of a woman's most obvious spiritual gift. It frustrates many to discover this. Gender restrictions with regard to spiritual gifts continue to be defined, defended, and debated. The question of a woman and her spiritual gifts is another of those theological issues that will be around for a long time.

I stated in the introduction to this book that it is not my purpose to attempt the last word on any issue affecting women. Rather, my purpose is to direct attention to what women can do in the absence of the final word. Thus it is not my intention to declare what women should or should not be doing in the church. Nor is it my primary goal to help women discover their gifts. Instead I address that group of women who find themselves in a peculiar position—aware of the nature of their gift, but finding themselves in a situation that limits the ways they can use it. I want to help them discover practical answers to this question: "How do I act responsibly while others are deciding what I'm supposed to be responsible about?"

Women generally choose either to accept things as they are or to devote themselves to fighting the system. But both of these courses seldom lead to satisfactory solutions.

Accepting Things As They Are

As part of the research for this book, I conducted a limited survey among women of various ages, church affiliations, and geographical locations. Among the questions I asked were these: "Do you find it difficult to exercise your gift because you are a woman?" and "If so, how are you handling this?"

The comments made by those who responded "yes" to my first question included these:

"I do what I can, and I don't exercise my gift all the time."

"I pray (about this) a lot."

"I don't get involved in my church."

A number who responded "no" nevertheless alluded to problems with gender restrictions:

"I always felt I lucked out. My major spiritual gifts are mercy and hospitality, very acceptable gifts for a woman in conservative Christendom."

"Mine happen to fall within the realm of those normally assigned to women."

For years, accepting things as they are has encompassed accepting inconsistencies within the Christian community. The evangelical world is notoriously blind to its inconsistencies, especially in the area of women and spiritual gifts. Tim Stafford demonstrated this inconsistency quite forcefully in a thought-provoking article, "Single Women: Doing the Job in Missions." Stafford asks long-overdue questions, and points out that the evangelical community is slow to emerge from that long-accepted chain of command, "God speaks to men, men speak to women, and women speak to children and foreigners."[1]

Stafford points to three important facts which demonstrate evangelical inconsistency: (1) Women missionaries are organizing churches, training men, and going into places where men dare not go. (2) People who totally reject the idea of women in the pastorate send thousands of single women out, and pay their salaries to start churches, teach the Bible, and administer programs. Says Stafford, "Every mission I know of has routinely assigned women to do a man's job."[2] (3) On the home front, these same capable, gifted women would be cleaning communion cups and taking flowers to the sick.

In the past women have accepted these inconsistencies, but in increasing numbers they now seek to use their gifts in roles previously denied them. Rather than accept things as they are, they choose to fight the system.

Fighting the System

Some women have come to view any gender restriction as an unwarranted, church-sanctioned roadblock designed to keep women in the background. They want to find a way to crash through that roadblock, thereby winning the privilege to minister as they please. Some have redefined the exercise of spiritual gifts as a "right" rather than a responsibility. In the struggle to win that right, attitude often becomes a greater roadblock than gender restriction.

Women are also finding that fighting the system is a time-consuming process, and accomplishes too little for their immediate need. As individuals, they still must face the question, "What do I do about my spiritual gift while the corporate battle is still being fought?"

The responsible woman doesn't settle for things as they are. Nor is she content with fighting the system. Instead she looks for creative, personal solutions to system-imposed problems.

A Revised Perspective Is Needed

Finding personal solutions requires a revised perspective. A woman must recognize two things in order to deal with problems surrounding the use of spiritual gifts. First, she must acknowledge that the church is in a transition period regarding this issue. Whatever changes have been made, whatever changes loom on the horizon, we are still in transition. Second, and most important, she must see that there can be no real coming to terms with the question of spiritual gifts aside from a knowledge of their purpose.

Transition is never easy. At best it's an ill-defined game where reasoning is at once challenged and obscured. The opposing players frequently engage in a series of violent reactions to one another.

Not long ago a young woman approached me after a luncheon at which I had spoken. She was concerned about several of her peers, recent female seminary graduates who were not accepted in their church. With a little probing I discovered her definition of being "not accepted" was that their church refused to allow women to be pastors. After further discussion I said to her, "Perhaps your friends should change their affiliation if exercising these gifts is that important to them."

"But that's not fair!" she challenged.

"Some churches will never accept women in certain areas of ministry," I emphasized. "To do so would be to go against the Scriptures as they interpret them. You must respect them for that. Other churches may change their position, but are yet in transition. Transitions take time and you can't skip steps."

Whether we like it or not, there is still a great gulf between seminary philosophy and local church practice. Increasingly seminaries are encouraging women to exercise their gifts, but earning a seminary degree—indeed having the support and sanction of the seminary—does not win for the female graduate a coveted ministerial position. Awards and endorsements notwithstanding, many mainline evangelical churches believe it is unscriptural to allow women to teach, let alone serve on the pastoral staff.

Not for Personal Fulfillment

What is the purpose of spiritual gifts?

> It was he who gave some to be apostles, some to be prophets, some to be evangelists, and some to be pastors and teachers, to prepare God's people for works of service, so that the body of Christ may be built up (Ephesians 4:11-12).

Clearly, spiritual gifts are not distributed for personal fulfillment, but for the edification of the body. Spiritual gifts are distributed by the Holy Spirit, at his discretion, for building up the body of Christ.

The purpose of the gifts is seldom discussed, yet once a woman recognizes their purpose, she can never simply determine "This is my spiritual gift, and I have a right to use it." (For that matter neither can men.) A spiritual gift is to be exercised in a manner that will be helpful to the body. To demand one's right to exercise that gift often proves divisive to the body and is therefore detrimental.

Several years ago while on an extended speaking tour, I had the opportunity to speak to a variety of churches. Meeting other members of the body of Christ was a delightful, stretching experience. However, because of my church background, I approached some moments with apprehension. One was the opportunity to speak at an early morning service. I was a bit uncomfortable with the implications of that.

The congregation's responsiveness put me at ease. They seemed not at all uncomfortable with me. Obviously they were accustomed to women participating in the service. For my presentation, I chose a study from the life of Moses. At noon the pastoral staff took me to lunch. Their kind remarks concerning my morning delivery were followed by a pointed question, "What's a nice lady like you doing in a church that does not ordain women?" or words to that effect.

After explaining that I am in my church because of personal conviction, I commented that any woman who seeks ordination should align herself with a sympathetic body rather than demand ordination at the expense of unity within the body. "Such demands defeat the purpose of spiritual gifts since spiritual gifts are given—"

"—for the edification of the body," finished one of my lunch partners. He was way ahead of me. We discovered that though we disagreed on practice, we had a clear consensus on the purpose of spiritual gifts.

Once the responsible Christian woman understands the purpose of the Spirit's gifts, she can better discern where and when to exercise them. The spiritually accountable woman recognizes that exercising one's gifts is not a right to be seized, but rather a responsibility to be discharged. Part of her responsibility is to determine when the exercise of her gifts benefits the body and when the exercise harms it.

Meeting Needs

In my research I ran across the personal account of one woman's struggle with the spiritual gift issue. She never tangled with the question theoretically, nor did she campaign for change at societal level. She was forced to deal with the issue because of a need which confronted her.

Married to a traveling minister, this woman found herself alone with her family in a neighborhood of great spiritual need. It never occurred to her, a woman, that she should try to meet her neighborhood's need. But she was greatly concerned for her children. She spent part of each day reading to them and instructing them in spiritual matters. One day one of her children told a friend, who told his parents, who begged to be included. Overnight she was leading a neighborhood Bible study of thirty to forty people.

At this point she became convinced that although she was neither man nor minister, she could do more than she was doing. She began to pray for the neighbors and to admonish them more when they came. The attendance doubled and then doubled again. Finally one night two hundred people came and others were turned away.

Conviction and responsibility notwithstanding, she was plagued with the usual questions about a woman and her spiritual gifts. Her husband wrote to her suggesting she allow one of the men to handle the lesson, but she pointed out that not a man among them was equipped for the job. Thus she continued to discharge what she considered to be her sacred responsibility.

Two things are notable from this incident. First, this woman did not use her gift out of compulsion to fulfill a role or to meet a need in her own life. Rather she did it out of a heavy sense of responsibility toward her neighbors' need.

Second, this incident is lifted from a letter dated almost three hundred years ago in which Susanna Wesley related her personal struggle with the spiritual gift issue.[3] We tend to think that the many questions regarding a woman and her spiritual gifts have been spawned by Christian feminists. In reality the proper use of spiritual gifts has concerned women for centuries. In Susanna Wesley's day and even before, women have been compelled by this same sense of responsibility, and they have looked for ways to discharge that responsibility.

What's a Woman to Do?

As each woman searches for answers to her personal dilemma, she must be sensitive to her particular situation. There will be times when she, like Susanna, will forge ahead in order to meet a need. But there may be other times when she must keep silent even in the face of need.

As a bride, I went with my husband to pioneer a work in a logging camp in Northern California. My husband deliberately sought out such a place of ministry though it meant he had to work six days per week in the mill to support us. He spent every evening preparing his weekly sermon or calling on parishioners. On Friday evenings we worked with the young people. There was little time left for Ken to take on other church-related jobs. So an untrained layman taught the adult Sunday school class.

The layman meant well. I did not doubt his intelligence, his sincerity, or his relationship with the Lord. But his biblical knowledge was negligible. In fact, he was completely untaught. One Sunday, following a prescribed lesson quarterly, he taught on the ark of God. Being familiar with but one ark in the Bible, he spent the entire hour trying to apply the quarterly's points on the ark of the covenant to Noah's ark.

Prior to this incident I had given little thought to the contention of many of our peers that women should never, under any circumstances, teach men (unless of course she went across the sea). But that day I began to look at the flaws in that line of thinking.

I was a Bible school graduate with experience teaching adults. I could have made a valuable contribution to that class. Yet I knew there was more to be considered.

Neither Ken nor I seriously considered the possibility of my teaching adults in that community. We felt it wouldn't be accepted. To force the issue could have proved detrimental to the overall ministry.

In subsequent churches I found myself teaching adults often—at their invitation. In unmistakable ways the Lord gave both opportunity and assurance that it was right for the body. In other words I knew my teaching would be beneficial in each situation.

Focusing on Personal Responsibility

Whether or not she finds herself in a church that encourages her to exercise all her gifts, the responsible woman remembers that spiritual gifts are given for a purpose: to edify the body of Christ, not to fulfill the need of the possessor.

1. Tim Stafford, "Single Women: Doing the Job in Missions," *Leadership*, vol. 3. no. 4; Fall, 1982, pp. 85-88.
2. Ibid.
3. Donald L. Kline, *Susanna Wesley: God's Catalyst for Revival* (Lima, Ohio: C.S.S. Publishing Company, 1980), pp. 17-19.

6

SPIRITUAL GIFTS: DISCOVERING YOUR OPTIONS

Are your ministry options limited?

Most women are painfully aware that their options are limited to the degree that their church practices gender restrictions. But whether a woman finds a place of ministry may be determined to an even greater degree by her reactions to those restrictions.

Recognition of the Holy Spirit's ministry in the administration of spiritual gifts is crucial. It is not enough to see that he distributes those gifts. We must also recognize that the Holy Spirit coordinates the ministry of those gifts.

I cannot explain precisely how this works, but I have observed the process in myself and in others. At a certain point in one's growth, in a certain period of life, the Holy Spirit chooses to use a believer in a specific area. The potential may have been there for years, but for one reason or another the gift was not previously used.

Women must recognize the limiting factor of the Holy Spirit. Without his ministry we have zero options. With his ministry we have whatever options he chooses to give us. Our response to this truth should be to commit our talents, our time, our gifts—indeed our life—to his disposal. Only then is a woman truly prepared to discover her ministry opportunities.

Her discovery involves preparation, availability, and creativity. These three keys must work together as a woman searches for options available to her.

Preparation Precedes Discovery

If a woman wants to discover her options, she must remember that her development as a believer is much more crucial than the development of her gifts. *Preparation* precedes discovery.

Sarah Jepson Coleman, popular speaker and author, stresses basic spiritual preparation that goes along with exercising spiritual gifts. On one occasion Sarah was approached by a noticeably handicapped woman. The woman communicated a desperate desire to discover her spiritual gift.

I remember listening to Sarah relate this story, and thinking to myself how one might advise such a woman—

Obviously this woman would be best fitted for behind-the-scenes work.

Obviously she would need help with self-esteem.

Obviously she couldn't expect anything spectacular.

Obviously . . .

But Sarah did not advise the woman along any of my "obvious" lines. She told her, "Get into the Word. Study. Be prepared. Then you pray and I'll pray, and we will see what God does."

A correspondence developed between the two. Word came to Sarah that her new friend was profiting from her study time. She had discovered the truth of the resurrection with the special dimension it held for people like herself. This was all a great joy, but her desire to discover her spiritual gift remained.

Sarah continued to pray. Her friend continued to pray—and to study.

Then one day the woman, crippled in body but prepared in spirit, accompanied a friend to the local veterans hospital. She wandered into a ward full of paraplegics. With little thought or plan, she went in and chatted with the men, all much more severely handicapped than herself. Soon she found herself sharing all she had learned about the resurrection. Not only did they listen, but when it was time for her to go they asked, "When can you come back?"

"Tomorrow," she replied, and with that her ministry was launched.

What if she had not been prepared? What if she had not experienced resurrection joy herself? Would she have recognized the opportunity when it came?

The Holy Spirit does not seem to use underdeveloped Christians who have "discovered their gifts." A woman must remember that her options will open up only as she is spiritually prepared.

More than Being at the Right Place at the Right Time

Availability is more than being in the right place at the right time. It is putting oneself at the Holy Spirit's disposal without attaching restrictions. Availability should never be contingent on perceived capability or on visibility.

While our spiritual gifts often lie within the scope of natural or acquired talents, they are seldom restricted to our capabilities. Often the area in which we use our spiritual gifts will stretch us. Few people called by God to accomplish a specific task ever feel qualified for it. We probably spend much of our lives exercising spiritual gifts in a way that is just beyond what we feel confident doing. Concern over capability should never restrict availability.

Because of gender restrictions surrounding the use of a woman's gifts, some women react by becoming more interested in visibility than in ministry. This desire for visibility is not a new problem. The mother of two of Jesus' disciples once approached him with the request that her sons be given the most prominent place in his kingdom.

A short time later, these two, as well as their ten companions, refused an option for ministry. At a no-host dinner where no one was available to wash the guests' dusty feet, not one disciple volunteered for the job.

In contrast to those who seek visibility are believers who suffer from "corner complex." Believing the only acceptable place to serve the Lord is in a corner where no one sees them, they insist on zero visibility—particularly for other Christians. If you must be seen, let it be while you are doing something for which you have no skills. That way, attention will be drawn to your dedication, not your skills. These people are never more happy than when they see an upper-management believer making clumsy attempts to use a hammer. It's as if proof of availability comes with a definite preference to attempt something for which one is completely unskilled.

There is, of course, a place for that kind of service. A skilled surgeon we know once spent a summer with other volunteers scrubbing floors at a remote youth camp. The experience turned his life around. But what a tragedy it would have been had he given up surgery to spend the rest of his life scrubbing floors!

It is wrong to refuse to do a necessary task because it's too menial. It's just as wrong to throw away a more visible gift in an effort to prove one's dedication. Visibility (or the lack of it) in using our spiritual gifts is not ours to choose; we decide neither for nor against it. We simply accept it. Making oneself available to the Holy Spirit means acknowledging that he is in control of the visibility factor.

Creative Initiative

To a great extent, finding one's options depends on spiritual factors. Both preparation and availability have spiritual dimensions which cannot be ignored. Practical suggestions for finding one's options are useless if the spiritual dimension is forgotten. If, however, the spiritual factors are kept in perspective, one can take practical steps toward discovering ministry options. This involves *creative initiative*.

Begin by making a list.

List the things you would like to do.

List the things you can do, including talents for which you don't see a need.

List the needs that have impressed you, even if you're convinced you personally can do nothing about them.

Use this list as a prayer guide. Ask God to provide the options he wants you to have. Don't be surprised if you find yourself using your gifts in all these areas.

In my study there hangs a well-worn baton, a souvenir not so much of my youth as of one unique opportunity during our ministry in the logging camp. In this isolated community of one hundred families, the public school system was academically sound but offered few frills. Ken and I attended the PTA meetings because it was the accepted thing to do whether or not one had children in school. At our first meeting, one of the mothers lamented that she wished the girls could have the opportunity to learn baton. "They miss so much being in a school this small," she commented.

Much to her delight, I volunteered on the spot to teach them. Four years on the high school twirling squad hadn't made me a skilled batonist, but I knew I could teach them the basics. "Suppose we have a club," I suggested. "We'll make it a Bible and baton club. Give me thirty minutes to teach them the Bible and I'll give them an hour's instruction on the baton."

Today the ancient baton is nothing more than a conversation piece. But I like to remember that it was used well, if briefly. There were few other opportunities for me in that particular place. But availability and creativity were keys that opened one door to minister on a small scale.

At times creative initiative involves carving out a niche. Sue Perlman is an executive secretary with Jews for Jesus. Her job takes her to far-flung places and thrusts her into top-level administrative tasks. I asked Sue how she would advise women who are looking for ministry options. She replied, "If there's an area in which a woman wants to exercise her gifts, she should be willing to start small and then carve out a niche—make a place, make herself indispensable."

Sometimes those steps lead into different and far wider challenges then one expects. Remember that many women who have a "ministry" were thrust into it. They did not enter by a well-laid plan of their own making, but nevertheless were busy carving out a niche.

Emma Dryer was such a woman. She helped Dwight L. Moody establish Moody Bible Institute. It has been said that without Emma's unfailing faithfulness and tremendous educational and organizational abilities, Moody Bible Institute would not exist today.[1]

As a young woman, Emma Dryer was greatly affected by the missionary and evangelistic movements of her day, volunteering to work in Bible classes for the poor. She was already involved in teaching women's classes in urban Chicago when she met Moody, who later referred to her as "one of the best teachers of the Word of God in the United States."

Moody was anxious to use Emma in his YWCA work. Primarily at his urging, Emma left school-teaching to become involved in full-time Christian work. For several years they discussed starting a school in Chicago, and in the end it was Emma who convinced Moody to do it. She called the meeting to organize what would become Moody Bible Institute, and took it upon herself to raise $750,000 for starting it. Now, a century later, we can all be thankful Emma Dryer found her niche.

"But I'm Housebound!"

"Am I missing my opportunities?" is a question often nagging the housebound woman. Prolonged illness (personal or that of another family member) and maternal duties are the chief reasons women find themselves staying at home. There she often becomes discouraged over her apparent lack of ministry options. She may feel that since she is largely unavailable to people, she is unavailable for ministry.

Martha Snell Nicholson and Amy Carmichael are notable examples of women who ministered to others while confined to bed. Their writings continue to minister to us today. In *Why Waste Your Illness?* contemporary author Mildred Tengbom quotes an anonymous friend: "It would seem that occasionally God allows illness for the benefit of others. To the atheist or agnostic, one of the best demonstrations of God is to see a child of his under stress. The difference in the life of the believer shows up best under pressure."[2] In some cases women have been thrust into a ministry of correspondence or intercessory prayer during a period of forced confinement when time hung heavy on their hands.

The mother of young children discovers early on that her time is completely occupied with her charges. Seldom will she find a quiet fifteen minutes to write a note of encouragement or to intercede for another believer. She may feel her ministry options are as limited as her world and become just as discouraged as the woman who is bedridden.

The responsible Christian mother acknowledges that child-rearing is a ministry in itself. She may get restless, even discouraged, but underneath it all she recognizes that for this period in her life, her primary ministry is the same as her primary work. Rather than look at her home as a place of confinement, she views it as a place to create a loving, caring atmosphere for rearing children.

At one time or another, most of us will experience prolonged periods of being housebound and, therefore, not available to people. During such periods we must remember that our primary responsibility is to be available to the Holy Spirit. We do not always understand how God will do it, but we can be sure he can minister through us even during housebound periods.

Professional Women and Ministry Options

As a minister's wife, I am acutely aware that we are losing much talent in our churches by failing to put people—men and women—to work in the areas of their gifts. Churches often don't recognize the potential contribution professional women could make to the ecclesiastical workforce. Professional women face peculiar problems when looking for ministry within their local churches. Skilled in finances, management, and legal matters, they may lack some of the more traditional womanly skills, or have little interest in those areas. When skilled laywomen face this on a continuing basis, they usually find their way into a parachurch organization which recognizes their potential.

"It's not that I mind doing that job," one woman remarked about a task thrust upon her, "it's just that I feel so clumsy about it." She has little skill for it, yet she willingly performs the prescribed task. But her most productive ministry is with a parachurch group where she regularly contributes hours of her time in an area for which she is gifted.

Women who find themselves in this position should observe two rules. (1) Be willing to do whatever task the Lord puts before you. (2) Commit your desire to serve in the area of your gifts to the Lord. Pray that he will open up the door. Then watch him work.

Boredom is a terrible enemy. When women are underchallenged they are bored and frustrated. A minister seldom stays where he is underchallenged. A businessman looks elsewhere. Women, too, refuse to be bored in their jobs.

But in our churches, some women continue to be underchallenged, aware of their boredom and angry because "my church won't do anything about it!" I believe that many gender restrictions are being lifted. One minister friend who pastors a 1,000-member "conservative" church said that they are now using women in areas of finances and management. He sees this as a definite trend with more changes to be expected.

Focusing on Personal Responsibility

Meanwhile, women—even women who fight to bring about change—must continue to find solutions to personal problems. While it is true that unresolved theological debates concerning females in ministry continue to limit options, nothing limits those options so much as a lack of preparation, availability, or creativity. The responsible woman recognizes that when these things fall into place, her options will become clear.

1. This information based on an article by Eric Fellman, "Emma Dryer: Visionary of a Bible School," in *Moody Monthly*, May 1985, pp. 81-84.
2. Mildred Tengbom, *Why Waste Your Illness?* (Minneapolis: Augsburg Publishing House, 1984), p. 122.

PART 4

MAKING A DIFFERENCE BEGINS WITH BEING MADE DIFFERENT

7

SELF-SUFFICIENCY: A CRUMBLING FACADE

Women are out to make a difference in their world. They are determined to demonstrate that they are capable, dependable, and resourceful. Christian women want the chance to prove they can be God's instruments in a changing world.

But this laudable desire has become tainted by the message that a woman can't do anything unless she is self-sufficient. Proponents of this message assume that each woman has a basic need to prove herself, to show someone somewhere that she can achieve her goals with or without help from others. They believe that if a woman takes charge of her own destiny, she will succeed—at what we aren't told!

A Secular Message: Control

Women are encouraged to take control through countless take-charge-of-your-life messages in the media. Every month we can find new "how to do it" magazine articles offering creative steps for seizing control of time, money, routine, wardrobe, and career advancement.

Small wonder we develop a determination to control our lives, to shape our own destinies—to become self-sufficient. The media convinces us that attention to the external will equip us for anything. Thus we eagerly grasp the promises offered through the self-help market. Recent media promotional pitches to women included these:

> The right clothes—are you making use of wardrobe power?
>
> The right communication skills—are you aggressive enough?
>
> The indispensable fitness program—do you feel good about your body?
>
> The right people network—are you making the most of your contacts?

Certainly, responsible women give attention to all these areas. The danger lies in crossing the line between responsibility and self-sufficiency—in the compulsion to control one's life and destiny. We forget that ultimately only God has that power.

When confronted with circumstances beyond our control, we don't like to admit there is nothing we can do. We dislike facing personal limitations. Yet all of us, women and men alike, have limitations like these:

An income less than $20,000 a year.

A body that tires easily because of polio.

Emotions scarred from being raised in a broken home.

Inadequate training for what we want to do.

Responsibilities that keep us in the home rather than busy doing things with people.

We may have limited resources . . . or limited understanding . . . or limited wisdom . . . or limited stamina, either physical or emotional or both. But our limitations render us dependent on God. Self-sufficiency robs us of that dependence.

The Changemakers

Contemporary Christian women are ploughing new ground, exercising gifts in areas previously denied them, filling positions once reserved for men, and paving the way for others who will follow.

As changemakers we must find that fine line between responsibility and self-sufficiency. We must keep a proper perspective on the struggle for change. We must acknowledge personal limitations. And we must never lose sight of our dependence on the One who has no limitations.

Responsibility concerns itself with getting the job done; self-sufficiency is concerned with proving oneself and maintaining a correct image. The woman who espouses self-sufficiency becomes very image-conscious. She is apologetic over any deviation from the perceived image of success. Preserving the image is not simply a question of designer labels or assorted success symbols. It hinges on male/female orientation in the work force and provokes such questions as "Should I make coffee on the job?" "Should I pick up the lunch tab?" "Should I defeminize my wardrobe?"

One friend confessed that for years she refused to wear pink. Such a feminine color threatened her executive image. She even felt compelled to explain that her pink powder room reflected her landlord's taste, not her own.

Some changemakers are satisfied that God is directing their plans, but they often find it difficult to deal with those who question the plans. "I know what God wants me to do; unfortunately, my friends haven't gotten the message." Thus what begins as determination turns to defensiveness, then to defiance. Without realizing it, a woman can become completely preoccupied with self-sufficiency, which only feeds the cycle of anger.

Acknowledging Limitations Leads to Inner Strength

In this morning's meeting of our women's Bible study group, Becky told us of a struggle that led to an encounter with God: "I was so self-sufficient in the area of finances," she said, "I was almost proud that we lived within our means, never piled up debts, and didn't get into the credit card routine." But then, she related, her husband's company transferred him to a new location, and they couldn't sell the house they left because of a slow real estate market. Double house payments soon exhausted resources. Bills piled up. Becky was reluctant to admit that she, a business major, couldn't find a way to resolve the problem.

"We had to turn it over to the Lord," she acknowledged, "but it was much harder for me than for my husband."

As I recall Becky's words I am conscious of my own conflict over control of events. I am a schedule-oriented person, the original time manager. I make good use of my time, know how to say "no" and, in general, control my working day. But for the past three months my routine has gone awry. Twice I have had surgery scheduled. Twice it has been postponed. (I dare to hope that the third time will be for real.) Contractors who promised a finished office a month ago are literally stumped at this point about how to finish the job. Books are piled everywhere waiting for completion of the new room. And if that isn't enough, I—who love absolute quiet when I write—must create while men walk to and fro upon my roof.

Like Becky, who met her limitation with the house market, I met mine with contractors and hospital schedules. In the midst of the confusion, I am reminded by the triple-pronged prayer for tranquillity that it takes courage to change what needs to be changed, grace to accept what cannot be changed, and a great deal of wisdom to discern the difference. Whether coping with daily routine or attempting to effect change, women need both courage and wisdom. When a Christian woman is able to recognize her limitations, she develops more than a superficial tranquillity. She develops inner strength.

Inner strength is enhanced, not diminished, by recognizing personal limitations. A tremendous sense of relief accompanies the acknowledgment, "I have no control over these events. God will have to take charge here."

There is no real strength apart from the knowledge of one's own limitations.

A Woman Who Made a Difference

There once lived a woman with that kind of strength. Throughout her life, Esther was shaped, prodded, and propelled by events outside her control. For starters, she was an orphan, raised by an older cousin. And if growing up without a mother's love was not sufficiently ego-shattering, she also became a human trophy of a conquering monarch—a prisoner of war. Along with a contingent of private citizens and government officials she was uprooted from her homeland and carried away into an alien environment.

Succeeding events continued to shape her destiny, and Esther rose to the highest female position in the Persian Kingdom. She became queen. In addition to her natural beauty, she acquired beautiful clothes, a crown, an honored position, and every material possession a woman could desire. She also managed to make King Ahasuerus indebted to herself by reporting a plotted attempt on his life that had been uncovered by Esther's guardian and cousin, Mordecai.

But a crisis came into her life, and Esther recognized that being the queen, living in the palace, and having a record of past loyalty couldn't buy her power with Ahasuerus. She couldn't control his decision.

In one sense Mordecai was responsible for the crisis. It was not of Esther's doing. But, as Mordecai so eloquently pointed out, she did have a responsibility in the matter.

Mordecai's refusal to bow down to Haman, an egotistical top official in the king's cabinet, angered Haman so much that he vowed to avenge his wounded ego by killing Mordecai and all his people. He contracted with the king to rid the kingdom of the Jewish populace. Mordecai went into mourning, complete with sackcloth and ashes.

In time news of the proposed pogrom reached Esther. Although she was forced to communicate with Mordecai through a messenger, they managed to express themselves rather well. Mordecai pointedly suggested that because of her closeness to the king she was the logical choice to intercede for the entire Jewish nation.

Esther just as pointedly replied that Ahasuerus had not sent for her in more than a month, and the whole world knew that no one—not even the queen—approached the king without a royal summons.

Mordecai would have none of it. "Don't think you will escape just because you're in the palace," he warned. "If you refuse to speak up, deliverance will come from another source, but you will die." Then he added the ultimate thought-provoker: "Who can say whether or not you have come to the palace for just such a time."

Was it possible that all the events that had shaped her destiny converged at this very hour? Could it be that the Jewish orphan had come to the palace specifically to prevent the Jews' destruction?

One thing is certain. When Esther accepted the challenge,

she did so with unclouded perception. She had no illusions about self-sufficiency. She knew her own resources were inadequate, and recognized her need for divine strength ("Pray and fast for me for three days," she told Mordecai). And she accepted her responsibility knowing she could not control the consequences—"If I perish," she said, "I perish."

But in the end it was the enemy, not Esther, who perished. The Jews were spared, and they all "had a good day" (Esther 8:17 KJV). Esther, acknowledging her limitations, had made a difference in her world.

Cultivating Inner Strength

The woman who wants to make a difference must seek inner strength instead of self-sufficiency. Inner strength develops in proportion to our recognition that God has no limitations, that he can overrule the events which invade our properly prioritized routines, forcing us to face personal limitations. Inner strength comes in realizing that, ultimately, only God can control our destiny.

Astronaut Millie Hughes-Fulford originally was scheduled to be a crew member on the Challenger space shuttle mission launched in January 1986. After the shuttle's explosion, she reflected on the tragedy, recalling that her first thoughts were for the crew. Then the thought hit her—this was her flight.

"It was a very sobering thought," she said. "You reflect back and realize that none of us have any real control over our future."[1] If a woman who explores the universe makes such an observation, how much more should we who worship the God who created that universe!

Focusing on Personal Responsibility

Self-sufficiency is an external facade. Eventually it will crumble. When self-sufficiency has exhausted its potential, inner strength will have just begun to work. It's all a matter of defining the right source. Self-sufficiency depends on personal potential. Inner strength is derived from God's potential.

Making a Difference

A responsible woman knows that her ability to face the challenges of her world flows from her relationship with Jesus Christ. Whether she concentrates on problems in her private world, or joins the corporate battle to win common rights, her strength stems from this Source.

1. *Marin Independent Journal*, January 30, 1986, p. A18.

8

ROLE VERSUS RELATIONSHIP: EVERY WOMAN'S CHOICE

Elaine Stedman once said, "Women do not find their fulfillment in a role. They find it in a relationship, and that relationship is with Jesus Christ."

A relationship with Christ should be a growing, deepening one, but it won't develop automatically. We must understand what growth involves if we are to experience it.

"How to Grow" is the subject of studies for new believers, studies for mature believers, and studies for believers who want to nurture other believers. In addition to books, there are tapes, video series, and seminars easily accessible to anyone who wants to learn. And yet we continue to have problems grasping the truth that true spiritual growth always involves a relationship. When we should be developing a relationship with Jesus Christ, all too often we find ourselves developing a role. Separating role from relationship is a challenge that constantly confronts the believer. We need to be transformed from within. We tend to outwardly conform to an image we imagine is imposed upon us.

The Pressure to Play a Role

From the beginning of our spiritual journey, we are pressured to master a role. The pressure process is all too predictable. As a new believer, a woman may be an eager pupil, anxious to find answers to endless questions, ready to express troubling doubts, honest about the gulf between what she is and what God wants her to be.

Then . . . someone puts expectations on her prematurely
  or a trusted mentor is shocked by her expressions
    of doubt
  or a new friend is impatient with her old habits
  or she grows impatient with herself in the
    time-consuming growth process.

"Doing" quickly becomes confused with "being." Three weeks into the Christian subculture is enough to convince a woman that she should always have the answers, always praise the Lord, and always smile. At the same time she is never to question, never to express doubts, and never to admit discouragement. Reality versus role becomes a constant battle.

Reality says, "I don't understand." Role demands, "Keep quiet about it."

Reality asks, "How do I know this to be true?" Role demands, "Bury that doubt."

Reality says, "They're putting expectations on me that I'm not ready for." Role demands, "Go along with it."

Like physical growth, spiritual growth takes time. A little girl may dress in her mother's clothes and mask behind Mother's makeup to play "grown-up." But she is still a little girl. She may become quite caught up in her role-playing at times. My niece at age three once disobeyed her mother and then, with hand on hip, she looked her mother in the eye and declared quite sternly, "I'm playing the mother today." But little girls do not hasten the growth process by superficial trappings or loud assertions. Neither do new believers become mature believers by performing a role.

We may play a role ever so fervently, but it is still a role. It is an outward appearance, a mask, a cover-up. The woman who succumbs to the pressure to play a role finds herself trying to keep up a facade while ignoring questions or doubts that refuse to go away. She almost convinces herself that even God does not see her innermost self. Her testimony may appear to be intact, but her spiritual integrity is disappearing.

Integrity Is Key

I perceive spiritual integrity as honesty in one's relationship with God. Without it, one does not grow a relationship, but simply performs a role.

A woman can demonstrate integrity in every area of life except in spiritual matters. She may be rigidly honest with employers, friends, and strangers and still lie fervently to herself about her spiritual status. When a woman finds herself mouthing phrases she does not yet mean, or pretending to be something she has not yet become, she is experiencing a loss of spiritual integrity.

Integrity revolutionized Peter's life. Before the resurrection he was impetuous and loudly loyal. But he made promises he could not keep. He readily confessed dedication which he failed to demonstrate. When he subsequently denied the Lord he professed to follow, he was forced to look inside himself. Discouraged, he gave it all up and went fishing.

In a meeting on the beach, the resurrected Jesus forced Peter to be honest about the level of his love for Christ. At Jesus' insistence, Peter bared his heart. He went no further in his declaration than his long-obscured integrity allowed. For the first time he was completely honest about what was in his heart. Jesus knew all along, but Peter's confession cleared the way to build a new relationship, and he became one of God's choicest servants.

We can all take courage from the record of Peter's confrontation. God is always ready to accept us where we are in order to bring us to where we ought to be.

Unmasked

An incident in a Sunday evening church service when I was thirteen brought me face to face with a temptation to wear a mask and attest to an untruth in order to hide my lack of dedication from others. The incident centered around two Bible clubs, a misunderstood altar call, and a pastor who encouraged spiritual integrity.

At the time I belonged to a Bible club for junior high and high school students. We called ourselves the Gethsemane Bible Club (GBC) because we met in a room directly behind a beautiful stained glass "Garden of Gethsemane" window. The GBC had but one purpose—to encourage young people to study, memorize, and understand the Bible. Without question, it was the single greatest influence in my early spiritual development.

The pastor didn't seem to care if we had two or twenty-two in the club. His only interest was in developing spiritually responsible young people. He expected us to complete our assignments and to be accountable for what we learned.

He urged us to support one another on the school ground where our peers did not necessarily respect our beliefs. Together we memorized Matthew 26:41—"Watch and pray, that ye enter not into temptation; the spirit indeed is willing, but the flesh is weak." We made that verse our motto and promised to help one another by a secret code. Whenever we observed a fellow club member weakening on campus we slipped alongside and whispered "41" (translation: "Remember Matthew 26:41").

One Sunday evening at the close of the service the pastor gave a strange invitation. "We have a club in this church called 'The Sons of Zebedee.' These young people have dedicated their lives to full-time Christian service. I would like them to come forward."

I had never heard of a club by that name. I was still guessing who those dedicated young people might be when I felt a poke in my ribs. "That's us," my friend whispered; "let's go." She began shoving me toward the aisle. In one mass movement the pew emptied itself of GBC members.

As I moved forward, I mentally protested any idea of my being "dedicated to full-time Christian service": *That's not me.* And to my knowledge, only one or two of the others had actually made such a commitment.

Nevertheless, every member of the GBC was soon standing before the congregation—a dozen or so bright-faced teenagers. Inwardly I seethed at my predicament. By standing in front of the church and the pastor, I was lying to them.

The worst was yet to come.

Realizing the misunderstanding, the pastor explained that he was not referring to the GBC. He then invited anyone who had not made such a commitment to be seated.

Only those who have grown up in a church where important spiritual decisions always involve walking down the aisle can possibly relate to this situation. It is never easy to make a public decision. It takes courage to rise from one's seat and proceed forward. In a sense you are making yourself accountable to all the people as you go on record as having made a decision to accept Christ, be baptized, join the church, commit your life to Christian service, or other decisions thought up by the minister. The aisle looks at least a mile long, and you feel as if every eye in the congregation is glued to you.

Try to imagine responding to the reverse invitation: "If you have not made this commitment, take your seat." I looked at my fellow club members. No one moved. I was sure most of my peers were more intent on saving face than on commitment. But I also knew I wasn't responsible for them. I was responsible only for me. Fighting back unwelcome tears, I walked back to my seat.

I was the only one. By my action I told everyone present I had no intention of committing my future to the Lord. I could not have felt more conspicuous had I screamed out my lack of dedication.

But I had to be honest with the Lord.

You can lie to the pastor. You can lie to the congregation. You can lie to your friends. You can even lie to yourself. But you cannot lie to the Lord. Even a thirteen-year-old can understand that. Standing or sitting, the Lord knew my heart. So I sat.

My pride was demolished, but my integrity was intact. I have always credited that pastor with sensitivity in saving face for me. He managed to smooth things over. More than that he commended me for honesty. In time I came to the place where I did indeed commit my life to the Lord, but I didn't make the decision from a desire to conform or to save face, but rather in response to persistent pressure from the Holy Spirit.

The incident still stands out as a crucial juncture in my spiritual growth. I recognize the vital contribution the pastor made by encouraging integrity. But I also recognize the choice was mine. I refused to play a role, and the decision freed me to grow an honest relationship with the Lord.

The responsible woman will seek to do away with any pretense which hinders the growth of her relationship with Jesus Christ.

Growing a Relationship Demands Commitment

Yet, integrity in and of itself does not induce growth.

Integrity admits there are spiritual levels not yet attained. Commitment keeps one reaching toward higher levels.

Integrity admits to questions, even doubts. Commitment keeps one searching for scriptural answers.

Integrity refuses to outwardly conform for the sake of saving face. Commitment drives one to seek inner transformation.

Commitment is an overused word and an unpracticed discipline. But as a key to spiritual growth, there is no substitute.

Our relationship with Jesus Christ matures in direct proportion to our grasp and application of his Word. Tim Stafford points out that for the ordinary layperson, Bible reading is a difficult spiritual discipline. He challenges leaders to help people succeed in personal Bible study routines. He lists discouragement, compounded by chronically crowded schedules, as one of the chief barriers to Bible reading. Among the suggested solutions, Stafford makes this statement, "People will not read the Bible regularly until they have the confidence that they can understand it for themselves."[1]

Commitment manifests itself through such spiritual disciplines as Bible study (private and directed), prayer, church attendance, and time spent with other believers. However, such exercises must be viewed as aids to growth, not as isolated goals. Until we understand what we study and apply it to our lives, the exercise is incomplete. Our relationship with Jesus Christ begins to flourish only as we pursue an understanding of the Bible and commit ourselves to obeying it.

Here are suggestions to aid your understanding of the Scriptures:

1. Read in a version you can easily understand.

2. Work with a portion which is manageable for you. It is better to read smaller amounts carefully and repeatedly than larger amounts superficially.

3. Read with the attitude, "This is supposed to be understood."

In other words, don't look at the Bible as some mystical book that gives you mysterious strength whether or not you comprehend it. Always look for the complete thought as you read—and the complete thought may be contained in three verses, ten verses, or a whole chapter. Train yourself to read by thought instead of by verse.

4. Use a study guide. Understanding the Scriptures is greatly facilitated through the use of prepared study guides. Go to your local Christian bookstore and ask to be shown what is available. Specify whether you want beginning, medium, or advanced level, and ask for those which use the inductive approach.

5. Find someone in your church who is a more advanced student, and ask her to help you on a regular basis.

6. Join a Bible study group. In Stafford's article he stated that his research found again and again that group Bible studies help people gain confidence and excitement about the Bible.

Focusing on Personal Responsibility

Calvin Miller has observed, "Learning can be a heavy burden." Miller writes with concern for new converts who get sidetracked by other things. "Their disciplined pursuit of God and the Bible are dropped. They trade a difficult discipleship for a religious image."[2]

Disciplined study is essential to the growth of one's relationship with the Lord. The responsible woman does not trade discipleship for religious image, neither does she accept a role as a substitute for a relationship. She commits herself to a growing relationship with Jesus Christ . . . and she'll make a difference in her world because she has been made different.

1. Tim Stafford, "Opening the Closed Book" in *Christianity Today*, April 4, 1986, pp. 25-28.
2. Calvin Miller, *A Hunger for Meaning* (Downers Grove, Illinois: InterVarsity Press, 1984), p. 54.

9

WOMAN TO WOMAN TO WOMAN

I have a small pin showing a red banner unfurled over a blue circle. The banner bears a hammer and sickle, and on the circle are the words "Intourist Moscow"—the name of the official Soviet tourist bureau. The pin is a souvenir of my husband's travel in the Soviet Union.

He often recalls that on that trip he bore another unmistakable mark of the western tourist: a short-sleeved shirt with button-down collar, for which a local citizen offered him four times what he paid for it in the United States. (He didn't sell it.)

When traveling in another country, we seldom blend into the local crowd. Clothing, hairstyle, and mannerisms often identify us long before our fractured uttering of a foreign tongue. We have the mark of a tourist.

The Many Marks of the Believer

From buttons to jewelry to bumper stickers, believers display tangible identification marks to alert the world that they belong to Jesus Christ. Some disdain all outward signs like these; others improve on them, such as whoever produced the bumper sticker reading, "If you love Jesus, tithe; anyone can honk!"

Many Christians testify that such outward marks can serve a good purpose. Peggy Robinson, a jewelery designer in Evanston, Illinois, placed a fish sign on her storefront to discourage requests for zodiacs and occult items which she refused to design. She said the sign was effective: The requests ceased after she displayed the fish.[1]

Whether or not we like these symbols of who we are, most of us understand the importance of the world knowing that we belong to Jesus Christ. Many of us respond to this need by composing a mental list of "Things to Do So that People Will Know I Belong to Jesus Christ."

Go to church regularly.
Clean up my life.
Be more patient with husband, children, and co-workers.

Go to the mission field.
Witness.
Be a fool for Christ's sake.

Conspicuously missing is the real mark of a follower of Jesus Christ: "By this all men will know that you are my disciples, if you love one another" (John 13:35). Three things intrigue me about this passage: the message conveyed by love among believers, that "love one another" is a commandment, and Jesus' timing in giving the commandment.

Loving other believers conveys that we belong to Jesus Christ, that we follow him, that we are his disciples. As far as the world is concerned, our love for Christ is gauged by our love for one another; our identity with him is marked by our loving identity with one another.

But the disciples were so concerned about Christ's going away that they failed to hear his going away message. Peter's response reveals that he measured love for Christ by something much more valiant than simple love for one another. He responded by asking, "Lord, where are you going?" and declaring "I'll follow you anywhere. I'll lay down my life for you." But he ignored the simple commandment Jesus had just spoken.

Like the disciples in the upper room, we often fail to understand the priority of this command. We understand the priority of loving him who first loved us, so we sing "I just want to love you, Lord." We understand the priority of friendship evangelism and so we sing "Love the world through me, Lord." Or we pray "Help me love the hurting, Lord," because we see the priority of reaching out to wounded believers.

All this is essential. But we can do it all and still not bear the mark of the disciple. Jesus is not talking about friendship evangelism here. Nor is he isolating the act of loving as something to be offered only to the hurting. He's talking about the essentialness of continual love among believers on an everyday basis, so the world may observe our love for him through our love for one another.

We have no time for nonessentials today. Too many essential programs demand our time. If the program allows for needy people, hurting people, or unbelieving people, we focus our attention on them because the program deals with important matters. But seldom do we see as essential the act of showing love to the average your-life-is-going-better-than-mine Christian.

Only when we love one another, woman to woman to woman, do we begin to bear the mark of a disciple, demonstrating our love for Christ.

COMMANDED TO LOVE

Jesus said in John 15:12, "My command is this: Love each other as I have loved you." This is one of the imperatives—the commands—of Jesus Christ, and none of them should ever be relegated to the low-priority category. His commands are distinguished from all else that he said.

You can begin to understand the necessity of this love whenever you observe a group of believers who seem to lack it. The program goes on, the missionary dollars go out, communion is regularly observed—but the identity mark isn't there. Personal needs aren't met, people don't get along, business meetings become verbal battlefields. One man who observed such a group for many years declared, "They ought to put on boxing gloves at that church and sell tickets."

When I was in my early thirties, my mother died after a year-long battle with cancer. There came a time when we knew that she had lost the battle. Soon she would be released from the shell that no longer resembled her and from the pain that had consumed her. My father had to weigh the issue of whether to tell her the prognosis of her illness. Did she perhaps suspect it already, and yet choose not to discuss it? Or if she didn't suspect it, should she be told so she could give any last messages to those she loved?

Words spoken on a death bed are viewed as singularly important to the one who speaks. Even our court system makes special allowances for these words. These were the kind of words Jesus spoke in John 13—17. This lengthy passage opens with John telling us that Jesus knew his hour had come. The end was near. It was his last Passover with his disciples. Judas had already left to betray Jesus. What final message did Jesus have for the eleven? What would he consider important enough to say at his last intimate time with them?

Many Good Friday sermons have been preached on Jesus' last words from the cross. Many sermons have been preached on his last words as he ascended to heaven. But the final message he spoke to his disciples before going to the cross are sometimes lost: "Love one another."

How Do I Love?

Identifying the need for love among believers does not necessarily lead to the genuine practice of love. There are many mystical, idealistic concepts surrounding the subject today.

Elisabeth Elliot observes that the word *love* has fallen on bad times: "In some Christian gatherings people are asked to turn around and look the person next to them full in the face, even if he is a perfect stranger, and say, with a broad smile and without the least trace of a blush, 'God loves you, and so do I,' and prove it by a hearty bear hug."[2]

It's often a good thing to be physically demonstrative, but love for one another is communicated not so much by turning to a pewmate and whispering the magic words as it is by our attitudes toward one another. Respect, kindness, selflessness, patience—all these demonstrate love. But love is conspicuously absent in the committee where tempers flare and unkind words are hurled. The real thing demonstrates self-control and mutual respect for one another.

Be hospitable. It is easy to see how the early-day believers had a unique testimony. When Jews began eating with Gentiles and slaves began worshiping with their masters, the outside world took notice of these Christians.

Donald L. Bubna writes:

> The custom of sharing meals at each other's houses must have dealt effectively with the pride and prejudice that was as prevalent in the first century as it is

> in our day. What Jew with any self-respect would ever think of eating with a barbarian? Or what slave would be invited to his master's table? Non-Christians who observed the believers saw the evidence of love. "Look how they love one another—they even *eat* together!"[3]

Today the church suffers from a lack of hospitality. Too many times we reserve social times only for those we know best, or enjoy being with. New people and people who don't fit the mold are left out. We fail to use hospitality as an expression of love.

Not all women are in a position to practice hospitality in the traditional sense. Schedules, financial consideration, and unsympathetic spouses are but a few of the barriers women may encounter. Still, every woman can find some way to show hospitality within the body. For starters we can take better advantage of built-in opportunities such as the weekly church service. Instead of being content to say in passing, "Hello, how are you?" we can earnestly and prayerfully seek to become better acquainted with fellow worshipers, to know them by name, to place family units together, and to pray for sensitivity toward those who need the encouragement of a warm smile or spoken word.

Hospitality in the home can come in many forms. Some women love to give formal dinner parties with all that goes with it—fresh flowers, the best china, a gourmet meal. Others prefer informal, impromptu after-church suppers. Some can handle a crowd. Others function best with just a few guests. If your guests are to be comfortable, you need to be comfortable, so don't take on more than you can handle. Decide what is best for you and then do it.

Hospitality builds bridges that can be built no other way. Ed and Mary attended a small close-knit church. When the church began to grow, the congregation no longer had that family feeling. Some people resisted the change and disliked no longer knowing or being known by everyone in the church. But Ed and Mary decided that every Sunday they would invite two or three couples over for a light snack after the evening service.

They made it a point to ask new people along with old members. In that way the new people got to know several couples, and it helped them feel welcomed into the body. Through their act of love Ed and Mary helped preserve a family feeling in a growing congregation.

Dispel some of the loneliness in the lives of others. I would guess that all women have problems with loneliness. They may not define their feeling as loneliness, but at times they feel set apart from others. The single mother feels set apart because she faces everything alone. The talented young executive feels set apart because her career labels her "different." The mother whose nest is newly emptied feels set apart because there is a sudden void. The young mother feels set apart because her only companions are all under three feet tall and speak with a vocabulary of twenty-five words or less.

Loneliness is not confined to "alone" people or "alone" times. It is triggered by different situations for different people. I suffer from crowd loneliness. Nothing makes me feel more alone, more a number without a face, than to be in a large group surrounded by peers, casual acquaintances, even close friends. I am not competitive in relationships, so when I'm in a situation where everyone seems to be competing for one another's attention, it has a negative effect on me.

A listening ear, a friendly note, your undivided attention after a church service—these little things mean a lot to a lonely person. In recent years I have observed one or two people who seem to have a special gift for spotting the loneliest person at a social gathering and responding with prolonged, undivided attention throughout the evening. This is an act of love.

Find time for others. We can't be intimate friends with everyone in the church. Likes and dislikes, common denominators, mutual needs draw people together. But even casual acquaintances should so feel the presence of love that they will know you are there for them.

You can actively promote loving friendship by acting as a catalyst among your circle of casual friends. The wider your knowledge of people, the more opportunities you will have to bring people together. Take the challenge of introducing one casual acquaintance to another simply because you know enough about each to know "You two ought to know one another."

Susan's schedule allows less time than she would like to spend with people, but she has been the instigator for several friendships through her "listen and learn" technique. She makes it a point to listen to people and to remember what they share about themselves. She consciously meets newcomers every week. In the past year she has set up the initial contact with four different pairs of women: a nurse with a nurse; an avid hiker with another hiker; a single young professional with another single; and a mother with a newly emptied nest with a mother who has survived the same experience. Susan multiplied her limited time and met the needs of others through a simple but much-needed exercise.

Most people view time in one of two ways—either "Every interruption is a divine appointment" or "My time is my greatest asset and I will not allow others to interrupt my plans." Irresponsibility can be found among women in both groups. Some cannot or will not seek ways to manage their time more wisely. Others are too rigid to recognize and accept necessary interruptions.

Rhoda was my interrupter for six months. Because I work at home I must control my telephone time. I do not have the luxury of spending hours on the phone with chitchat. Most of my friends are aware of this. Rhoda may have been aware of it, but her needs were too great to accept it. She became a compulsive phoner, calling as her needs demanded. I recognized that Rhoda had a need. I tolerated her frequent, lengthy disruptions of the daily routine because I sensed that need. If I couldn't be there for her, who would be?

Oswald Chambers writes, "God continually introduces us to people for whom we have no affinity, and unless we are worshiping God, the most natural thing to do is to treat them heartlessly, to give them a text like the jab of a spear, or leave them with a rapped-out counsel of God and go. A heartless Christian must be a terrible grief to Our Lord."[4]

Controlling time is important, but there are times when we

must set schedules aside and make room for that person who needs us.

Cultivate friendships. Perhaps you need a friend. Remember that the first steps in cultivating a friendship are usually one-sided: It grows after one person begins by actively reaching out, rather than being a spontaneous, chemistry-related happening between both persons.

Proverbs 18:24 declares that the one who would have friends must show himself friendly. To have a friend, you must be a friend. To gain a friend, you must offer friendship. Perhaps you and your husband need Christian fellowship with other couples. What can you do to help bring this about? Look around your circle of acquaintances. Get to know more about people. Be willing to make the first move to cultivate a friendship with one or more couples. Go into it with a two-sided prayer, "God, give me friends—and help me be a friend to them."

If schedules are hard to mesh, don't overlook the obvious. Is your church having a social event? Call another couple and invite them to join you. Is your evening service at an early time slot? Light refreshment after church makes it easy on the cook and the budget. It also is less intimidating than entertaining for an entire evening.

Be available. For several years I have been involved in a writing project with my father. He has shared his roots in a lengthy account of his early life. In his day friendship was a necessary thing. Neighbors depended on neighbors. They helped one another with the planting and the quilting. They assisted in the business of birthing and dying and all the illnesses in between.

Today in our more hurried times the concrete need for one another has diminished, but the emotional need still is there. Everyone needs a friend to count on. We can look back and see how in times of trauma a friend made the difference.

In a dark period of illness during our seminary days, Ruth was there for me. She had other friends who could have offered her something in return for her friendship. But she committed herself to me, who had nothing but tears and despair. In more recent days of sorrow surrounding the illness and death of our first grandchild, there were two who just sat with me. They brought lunch or a croissant from the bakery and just sat. There was the friend from Germany who called and the one from Kansas who wrote, "I'm here saying 'Hurray for Joy.'" They made a difference for me.

Focusing on Personal Responsibility

We've all needed someone to count on. But do we take the responsibility to *be* someone to count on? With all our attention on roles and rights, are we losing sight of the relationships in our lives?

Women may continue to struggle with barriers in their attempts to overcome gender restrictions. But a responsible woman realizes there is no barrier to exercising love. Perhaps when all else is said, this is the greatest ministry priority women can have. It was, after all, the ministry which was most on the heart of our Lord in his last intimate meeting with his closest followers.

1. Summarized from *Christian Women at Work* by Patricia A. Ward and Martha G. Stout (Grand Rapids: Zondervan, 1981), p. 213.
2. Elisabeth Elliot, *Passion and Purity* (Old Tappan, New Jersey: Revell, 1984), p. 9.
3. Donald L. Bubna with Sarah Ricketts, *Building People through a Caring, Sharing Fellowship* (Wheaton, Illinois: Tyndale, 1978), p. 60.
4. Oswald Chambers, *My Utmost for His Highest* (New York: Dodd, Mead, and Company, 1935), p. 92.

CONCLUSION: FINDING MEANINGFUL FUNCTION IN A MALFUNCTIONING SOCIETY

No generation of women has ever been so acutely aware as our own of the emptiness that accompanies work without worth.

In the past women felt pressured toward self-discovery, and responded by searching for meaningful existence. Today women feel pressured toward self-achievement and respond by searching for meaningful function. Questions of "Who am I?" have given way to "Is there meaning in what I do?" Career women and homemakers alike experience this common need: to find purpose in one's task.

Many conclude that the primary barrier to meaningful function is a system which discriminates against women. They say, "Let's make the system work so we can work within the system." In reality, trying to make the system work usually leads to more frustration than function. And inevitably, for a few, the right to function becomes more important than function itself.

In my opinion Christian leaders have not adequately confronted the implications of women challenging the system. Many Christian women feel an awareness of inequality. Discontentment with things as they are has settled in. Only the naive expect this discontentment to go away. Women have pried open a door and they intend to enter. They are not going through a phase. They are in transition, and coming generations of women will not easily settle for meaningless routine.

Having stipulated that the Christian community as a whole does have a responsibility to grapple with these issues, I return to the focus of this book: the responsibility of the individual.

Defining Meaningful Function

The Christian woman who searches for meaningful function within her circle of influence must define what she is looking for. We are surrounded by imagemakers, both in secular and Christian society, who try to determine women's acceptable function.

The imagemakers communicate that the right role brings meaningful function. Thus women search for the perfect role: stimulating but not too demanding, challenging but not impossible, affirming yet not consuming.

Kay writes of her struggle with the superwoman image projected by the media: "Social pressures of women's roles in society, especially reflected in the media, portray the woman as an all-capable, beautiful, handle-everything type of person with no problems." Separating oneself from this imposed image can be a major hurdle in defining meaningful function.

Perhaps because of the imagemakers, women view meaningful function as being without drudgery and coming very close to the dreams which keep them going—dreams of reaching one's full potential, of earning the public and private respect of one's peers. In reality, most meaningful function occurs at some point between drudgery and dreams, often falling short of our highest dreams and always including a certain amount of drudgery.

Some years ago my husband made a decision which greatly affected my writing career. After attending a leadership conference at which the speaker emphasized that employees are more productive when they see purpose in their task, Ken suggested rather strongly that I resign my church secretary position. I was an experienced secretary and small-office manager, and I had performed my task to everyone's satisfaction. But my husband became convinced the job was not challenging enough for me—too routine and without much purpose. He suggested the time had come for me to devote full time to writing.

From the beginning I found more joy and a greater sense of accomplishment in my writing than I had in the office routine, but to end the story there is to miss the point. Writing is not without drudgery and it is certainly not the stuff of which dreams are made. There are days when I hate what I do. Yet writing has purpose for me, and that's what makes it meaningful function.

Meaningful function is more easily defined as a woman asks herself, "What has purpose for me?" The imagemakers have so influenced our thinking that women have forgotten the very personal nature of meaningful function. What is important to one may be of little importance to another. Laurie writes, "I need to feel that what I do is worthwhile. . . . When I was younger, I needed appreciation more. Now I realize that many jobs are unnoticed, but as long as I can see their value, I'm okay."

Only as we recognize the importance of individuality in defining meaningful function will we be able to separate ourselves from the expectations imposed by the imagemakers.

For the Christian the source of all meaning in life is Jesus Christ. It's therefore fruitless to attempt to find meaningful function apart from a meaningful relationship with him. From that relationship function is at once directed and empowered. All other suggestions for discovering meaningful function presuppose that this relationship is thriving.

Function Within the Body of Christ

In the survey conducted as part of my research, I asked the question, "What, if anything, would you like to see changed in your church regarding policy or practice toward women?" The answers ranged from contented ("Nothing") to caustic ("My church treats me as if I did not have good sense.") In between there were a significant number who communicated something akin to desperation about the lack of opportunity for meaningful function within their church. Most expressed support of their church in spite of disagreement. One woman wrote, "In spite of disappointment, I believe it's important that we as a family support our church."

Our ability to find meaningful function within the church is measurably affected by the degree to which we understand how the body of Christ is intended to function. According to Scripture, many restrictions accompany function. We are told nothing to indicate that believers (male or female) have unlimited options for function within the body.

In support of unrestricted female function in the church, Galatians 3:28 is frequently quoted: "There is neither Jew nor Greek, slave nor free, male nor female, for you are all one in Christ Jesus." In this brief statement Paul erased class distinction, race distinction, and gender distinction. Although many use this passage to argue that we all have the same function (or at least are entitled to the same function), I suspect the passage has little to do with function. Paul is concerned with relationships within the body of Christ. He is calling believers to a change of attitude rather than a literal change of status.

A comparison of similar instruction in other of Paul's letters clarifies his intent (1 Corinthians 7, Ephesians 5-6, Colossians 3-4, 1 Timothy 6, and Titus 2). In declaring that no divisions existed in Christ, Paul did not put an end to those divisions in society. Instead he demanded of all believers a change in attitude on the basis of their standing in Christ. Men were to love their wives; women were to respond with respect. Masters were to treat slaves kindly; slaves were never to use their common spiritual identification as an excuse to show disrespect to their owners. These passages teach us much about coexistence and attitude, but they do not speak directly to functional options within the body.

For a more accurate picture of how the body of Christ functions, we must turn to 1 Corinthians 12.

> For the body is not one member, but many. If the foot shall say, Because I am not a hand, I am not of the body; is it therefore not of the body? And if the ear shall say, Because I am not the eye, I am not of the body; is it therefore not of the body? If the whole body were an eye, where were the hearing? If the whole were hearing, where were the smelling? But now hath God set the members every one of them in the body, as it hath pleased him. . . . Now are they many members, yet but one body (12:14-20 KJV).

In this passage Paul underscores that we are all one in Christ, placed into the body by one Spirit. Even as he points to the commonality of the believers in relationship, he instructs them on their individuality in function.

The body of Christ is divinely designed as an interdependent system. Ideally, the people within the system function as a unit. Paul compares this to the human body where parts have individual purpose but are incomplete apart from the whole.

In the body of Christ, function is largely determined by the Holy Spirit, as we saw in chapter 6. We don't choose. We are directed as the Holy Spirit chooses.

Our spiritual qualifications and our circumstances also restrict our function. For example, the slave's circumstances gave him fewer options than a free man. But that did not relieve him of spiritual and ministry responsibilities. No one is excused from function. We don't choose whether or not to function—it is our responsibility.

Confronting Malfunction

The church doesn't always function as a body—its parts don't always function in unity with the whole. When the foot decides it wants to be a hand, the whole body suffers. When overseers fail to oversee, the body suffers. And when churches fail to consider how a woman can best function within the interdependent system, a segment of the body suffers.

Many women perceive the church as a malfunctioning system—an institution regrettably behind, a place to worship God but not serve him. Some become preoccupied with correcting the system. The right to assume responsibility becomes more important than responsibility itself. One woman commented, "I don't even want to do that job. I just resent being told that I can't do it because I'm a woman."

Another woman asked me, "Why would God give a woman a gift if he didn't intend for her to use it?" Before dealing with the question I think we must address two errors communicated through the question. (1) The questioner assumes that women are the only ones who have gifts that aren't used. (2) The questioner assumes that if a gift isn't being used *now*,it will never be used.

I remember in our student days that a similar question frequently arose concerning gifted men—should they go to the mission field where their great skills as an organist, pianist, or soloist would be "wasted?" I think we must concede that there are times when both men and women will find their primary gifts not being used. We must also remember that we do not know what plans God has for the future. The final chapter has yet to be written concerning God's use of our gifts.

My friend Alma commented on the possible reasons God allows our gifts to go unused for the time being. "Jesus' example makes me realize that greatness lies in servanthood, not in accolades. To the extent that church leadership hinders my exercise of certain gifts, I consider that there must be a lesson for me in dealing with the hindrance or that God needs another gift used just then." Alma admits that some spiritual gifts are more difficult than others for a woman to exercise, but that there will be opportunities even for those if she exercises patience.

My friend Laurie agrees.

Laurie is self-motivated. When it comes to private Bible study she has both the knowledge and the discipline that makes for a good student. Not surprisingly, she is an excellent teacher—but her church situation makes it difficult for her to function as a teacher. "How have you handled this?" I asked.

"I pray a lot," she replied, "and I teach women how to study when I'm asked. Since only women ask for instruction, I don't have to face the dilemma of teaching men." Currently her teaching is confined to one-on-one instruction. Although she could handle a large class, she has found both joy and purpose in working with individuals. She frequently counsels younger untrained women who are unable to find answers they need in the Scriptures. Objectivity permits Alma and Laurie to continue to enjoy fellowship and worship in their respective churches. Such benefits are lost on those women who see only flaws in the church.

The responsible woman gives herself frequent attitude checks. She strives to focus on what she *can* do rather than on what she can't.

Prayer, Patience, and Creativity

For Laurie and Alma, prayer, patience, and the ability to be creative have led to meaningful function. Women can experience meaningful function in spite of seemingly impenetrable barriers—but probably not without these vital keys.

A call to prayer and patience does not mean women should always compliantly accept gender restrictions which they believe are unfair. It does mean that there are times when a woman must commit those restrictions to the Lord and wait to see what he will do. But there are also times when a woman should communicate with her minister about perceived malfunction. As a minister's wife I can say that women seldom do this. This is the most neglected means of effecting change—most ministers welcome creative input from lay people, both men and women.

Your minister needs to hear specifically what you perceive as malfunction. If you expect action, he also needs to hear positive input on possible solutions. It may be you will plant a seed which will lead to change. It may be you will gain new insight which will change your own thinking. In either case, the success of the contact lies in your ability to communicate rationally and intelligently about the perceived problem.

An attempt to make creative compromises should precede a decision to change churches. Certainly there are legitimate reasons to change churches, but I don't believe this is the first alternative for women who are looking to use their gifts. If you agree doctrinally and if other needs are being met, changing churches is not the answer. Ask yourself if there are obvious solutions. If your church won't allow you to teach where men are present, will it allow you to teach women? If you can't get involved in administration at the top level, can you administer at a lower level? If you are discouraged from participating in a program, can you get involved with people?

The church needs people to get involved with other people. Sometimes we need to enlarge our vision on what constitutes body function.

Enlarging Our Vision

Opportunities abound for believers with vision.

In one of our former churches I met Rhonda, a Bible college graduate who confided in me that her fondest dream was to be a minister's wife. Her husband headed a large corporation and their sphere of influence in the community was potentially far-reaching. Rhonda dreaded every social contact with her husband's business associates. "Their lifestyle is so different, we have nothing in common," she said. She confessed that her dream of the ministry represented an escape from their situation and a "real chance to serve the Lord."

Then one day Rhonda and her husband caught a vision. They saw that their situation afforded them opportunities no minister had. They began to invest time and effort into making friends among their business associates. The friendship network led to an extremely fruitful ministry. Many lives were redirected and several churches reaped the benefits of their labors.

Ken and I live now in a high-tech, upwardly mobile area. Banks appear on every corner while fast-food operations are hard to find. It is not the most fertile ground for churches. Churches from denominations which are booming elsewhere struggle here just to survive. That which attracts crowds in another area fails to gain a hearing here.

One of the most creative efforts to reach the community is being carried on by a group of women with a vision. All are active church members; most are involved in a neighborhood outreach. As a group they frequently sponsor country club luncheons or public meetings featuring nationally known Christian women speakers. These women combine their administrative and artistic skills. They plan and execute every detail of their operation. They pray over the guest lists. I have observed their dedication and their vision. As examples of women who have taken the initiative to find meaningful function, they are making a valuable contribution to the body of Christ.

Focusing on Personal Responsibility

No generation of believers has ever functioned within a flawless system. Since the beginning of the church, Christians have had to face systems which were politically hostile and fraught with theological error. Responsible believers have found ways to function under the most negative circumstances.

Today responsible women make necessary choices as they determine before the Lord how he would have them function. As they concern themselves with finding meaningful function in a malfunctioning system, some will lobby for change, some will make creative compromises and wait for further opportunities, some will find that restriction leads to redirection. In some cases women will find their most meaningful function outside the normal program of the church.

Whatever route she chooses, the responsible woman will pay careful attention to attitude as she commits her situation to the Lord.

If I must serve without accolades,
may I also serve without division:
if not in the way I would choose,
then in the way you redirect;
if not within my church program
then wherever you open the door.

With singleness of purpose, the responsible woman declares with Joshua of old,

"As for me . . . I will serve the Lord."